"... an unmarried man is concerned about the Lord's affairs—how he can please the Lord....An unmarried woman...is concerned about the Lord's affairs: her aim is to be devoted in both body and spirit."
1 Corinthians 7:32, 34 (NIV)

The apostle Paul's advice to single men and women is as applicable today as it was when he first wrote these words. *Movers and Shapers* introduces you to single men and women who were compelled by love to commit themselves wholeheartedly to God's service. None took their commitment lightly; each sacrificed marriage, health, prestige, wealth, or personal comfort in order to obey the Lord's calling. Yet at the end of their lives, every servant was able to say that he or she made the best possible choice as each knew the happiness and peace of an intimate walk with Jesus Christ. Through these interesting vignettes, you will learn lessons in faith, obedience, patience, hope, and the Lord's ability to provide all of your needs.

MOVERS
& Shapers

HAROLD IVAN SMITH

FLEMING H. REVELL COMPANY
OLD TAPPAN, NEW JERSEY

Unless otherwise identified, Scripture quotations in this book are taken from the King James Version of the Bible.

Scripture quotations identified NIV are taken from the HOLY BIBLE: NEW INTERNATIONAL VERSION. Copyright © 1973, 1978 by the International Bible Society. Used by permission of Zondervan Bible Publishers.

Excerpts from DAVID BRAINERD BELOVED YANKEE by David Wynbeek, copyright © 1961 William B. Eerdmans Publishing Co. Used by permission.

Quotations from *The New Lottie Moon Story* by Catherine Allen. Copyright © 1980 Broadman Press. All rights reserved. Used by permission.

Excerpts from THE FIVE SILENT YEARS OF CORRIE TEN BOOM by Pamela Rosewell. Copyright © 1986 by The Zondervan Corporation. Used by permission.

Quotes taken from HENRIETTA MEARS AND HOW SHE DID IT by Ethel May Baldwin and David Benson. Copyright © 1966 by Gospel Light Publications. Used by permission.

Library of Congress Cataloging-in-Publication Data
Smith, Harold Ivan, 1947–
    Movers and shapers.
    Bibliography: p.
    1. Christian biography.   2. Single people— Biography.   I. Title.
BR1702.S63   1987   280'.092'2   [B]   87-16438
ISBN   0-8007-5261-9

Copyright © 1988 by Harold Ivan Smith
Published by the Fleming H. Revell Company
Old Tappan, New Jersey 07675
Printed in the United States of America

Contents

We who dwell in the twentieth century are experiencing the collapse of faith in the rival who was to replace Him: man. Poets applaud the absurd, novelists explore the decadent, and men prostrate themselves before the deities of lust and power. Our obsession is with human flesh. . . . Daily we are bombarded by lurid reports of the mass-killer, the rapist, and the corrupt bureaucrat. The fantasies of even little children are now peopled with perverts and the radiated dead. *Who will speak of those who do [did] justice, love mercy and walk humbly?* [Italics added.]

—*Rabbi Joshua Herschel*

*Although history was made by people
who are now dead
we must never forget
that they were alive when they made it!*

—*Philip Guedalla*

Introduction

This American habit of destroying our heroes after we've built them up sickens me.

—Barbra Streisand

Once upon a time, Americans believed in heroes—whether presidents, military figures, business tycoons, or ministers. Innocence prevailed in the mind of the American public concerning those who led. We obeyed them because we had respect for them and for their offices.

But in the aftermath of Vietnam and Watergate, and more recently "Irangate," there has been an enormous erosion of confidence in public figures, no doubt reflected in the decline of voter turnout, the significant menace of voter apathy, the indictment of a vice president, the resignation of a president to avoid impeachment, to say nothing of reports of escapades and wrong-doings by members of Congress. The highly sophisticated news media seem determined to sift every detail, offering tidbits on the evening news as appetizers for our evening meals.

A mood exists, a hunger to debunk, to demyth, to

dethrone. Yet the Christian, in reading Hebrews 11:33–38, finds a virtual "Who's Who" of the Christian faith. These giants

> . . . conquered kingdoms, administered justice, and gained what was promised . . . shut the mouths of lions, quenched the fury of the flames, and escaped the edge of the sword; whose weakness was turned to strength; and who became powerful in battle and routed foreign armies. . . . Others were tortured and refused to be released, so that they might gain a better resurrection. Some faced jeers and flogging, while still others were chained and put in prison . . . put to death by the sword. They went about in sheepskins and goatskins, destitute, persecuted and mistreated—the world was not worthy of them . . . (NIV).

Over the past months, I've sat in musty libraries, reading journals and diaries and letters, looking for hints or clues—anything that would help me understand the single saints included in this book. At times, I've felt like a detective: prying, prodding—only to push back from the table in amazement at some fact or detail.

They were the movers and shapers of society. Without the restraints of family they were able to prove the validity of Paul's contention in 1 Corinthians 7:32–34, "An unmarried adult is concerned about the Lord's affairs—how to please the Lord. But married adults are concerned about the affairs of this world—how to please their mates, and their interests are divided" (my paraphrase).

These single saints abandoned the quest for "the American dream" in order to pursue God's dream wholeheartedly.

Certainly they were mocked, ridiculed, harassed, yet they pursued, obediently. They dared explore the perimeters of their worlds, giving extra time and effort that paid remarkable results—time that otherwise would have gone to families.

As a result of their sacrifice, the kingdom of God has been enlarged, diseases have been conquered, injustices resolved, unjust regimes toppled, and dreams underwritten.

Because they lived, the world has never been the same.

I was amazed that fear was conspicuously absent from their lives. In his book *How to Make a Habit of Succeeding*, Napoleon Hill identified several common basic fears of mankind: poverty, criticism, ill health, loss of love, old age, loss of liberty, death.

As you read the following pages, keep that list in the forefront of your mind. While such fears may influence contemporary single adults, there is no evidence that these shapers and movers allowed such to block or restrain their obedience.

Some years ago, W. L. Howse wrote a book called *The Church Staff and Its Workers*. In it he offered a list of leadership qualifications for Christian workers. You will find these in the lives of the shapers and movers:

1. Called of God

2. Love for people

3. Physical energy

4. Sense of purpose and mission

5. Patience and self-control

6. Willingness to study and work

7. Ability to adjust

8. Ability to cooperate

9. Balanced judgment and tact

10. Sense of humor

11. Ability to take criticism

12. Strong in the faith

13. Effective in prayer

What is clear is that most of these individuals faced and conquered the significant loss of love: Lillian Trasher returned her engagement ring ten days before the wedding; Rebecca Eaton said no to Luther Rice; Belle Bennett could have had her "pick" of the men; David Brainerd died before he could marry Jerusha Edwards. But the shapers and movers did not allow their marital status—or lack of status—in a marriage-centric world to keep them from obeying. They all sought *first* the kingdom of God.

Yet one fear did taunt them: a fear of being mediocre, of disappointing or disobeying God. They disciplined their lives and found such deep spiritual foundations in prayer, in the Word, in fellowship that they did not waver, even in the midst of plagues, controversies, wars, and political uprisings.

We must not envy them but must seek to absorb from their lives that which could nourish our dreams, our visions, that which could encourage our obedience.

Certainly they had regrets, disappointments, hardships

en route to sainthood, but even their regrets came under the rigors of discipline.

They all perceived life as a precious gift.

In the next pages, I invite you not to enshrine them in a "Single Adult Hall of Fame"—there are far too many such institutions now. Each of these individuals learned what Fulton Sheen knew, that "the humble man recognizes that titles, honors, positions, glory are all external to himself, and could be lost in a moment."

Rather, let us read and listen and wonder. For though they are dead, yet they speak, they call, they dare single adults to discover God's dream in this season called singleness.

1.

Lillian Trasher

BORN: September 27, 1887

PROFESSION: Missionary

DIED: December 17, 1961

*"I'*ll wait for you, Lily," the tall young preacher declared as he stared in disbelief at his fiancée.

"But what could I do in one or two years?" Lillian responded.

"Then take three or four years—"

"No, Tom, this is good-bye. Now. For all time." Little did Lillian Trasher realize all that ending an engagement to a man she loved would come to mean.

But years later, as she lay in the heat of Assiout, Egypt, as she heard the happy sounds of 1,200 children, she died knowing that she had made the right choice.

Lillian Trasher grew up in Brunswick, Georgia. There was nothing extraordinary about her childhood except for a prayer she said while playing in the woods one day. She knelt by a log, handed the Lord a bunch of flowers, and prayed, "Lord, if ever I can do anything for You, just let me know and I'll do it."[1]

Years later, while waiting for a train in Asheville, North Carolina, Lillian met Miss Maggie Perry, who ran an orphanage in nearby Marion. Miss Perry, who had no "supporters" other than the Lord, invited Lillian to come to work at the orphanage. Lillian promised to think about it. Little did she know that Miss Perry would give her training for her entire life's work.

A few months later, Lillian arrived at the Elhanah Training Institute, where she immersed herself in sewing, cooking, taking care of newborn babies, and supervising large numbers of children—orphans no one but Miss Maggie wanted. There Lillian learned "how to trust God for the needs of everyday life. I had no money at all and no one sent me any. Neither did I write to people about my needs (which were indeed many). When my shoes wore out, Miss Perry had no money to buy me another pair. Well, someone sent in a box of old clothes and there was a pair of men's shoes in the box. They were not new but they were better than what I had on, so I asked Miss Perry if I might have them."

"Well, my dear, of course," Miss Perry answered, "but they are men's shoes."

"It took more than that to bother me," Lillian reported. "The lack of a pair of shoes was not going to make me leave or write home for money."[2]

Lillian attended God's Bible School in Cincinnati, pastored a church in Dahlonega, Georgia, traveled in evangelistic work in Kentucky, and then, in 1909, returned to Marion, North Carolina, where she became engaged.

Lillian had been praying for a call to the mission field—a common prayer among single women in this era—but, as Lillian later laughed, the Lord wasn't cooperating. Apparently, "He wanted to wait until I had entirely given up the idea and planned a different course for my life. Then He let me have the privilege of giving up all for Him."[3]

Ten days remained before her wedding when Lillian accompanied Miss Perry to hear a missionary from India. Deeply touched by the message, Lillian cried through the service, all the way back to the orphanage and into the night. Finally Miss Perry knocked on her door to ask what was wrong.

"Nothing is wrong," Lillian answered, "except I am engaged to marry the most wonderful young man in the world and I can't marry him."

Miss Perry, a bit of a matchmaker, insisted they were the perfect couple and didn't understand Lillian's trouble.

"God has called me to Africa," Lillian explained amidst her tears, "and I must obey."

There was no question in Lillian's mind. She had to put God first. Knowing little about where she was to go, she gathered her few possessions and a few dollars and headed for a holiness missionary convention in Pittsburgh. She was sure God would provide the means, just as He had provided the call. And He did. In a short time she arrived in Brooklyn, on her way to Egypt. Just before departure, Lillian's beloved sister Jenny joined her and, as friends prayed for the two single women in their cabin, someone urged Lillian to ask for a promise. Lillian opened her Bible and stared at Acts 7:34: "I have seen, I have seen the affliction of my people which is in Egypt, and I have heard their groaning, and am come down to deliver them. And now come, I will send thee into Egypt."

When the two sisters docked in Alexandria, they traveled by train to Cairo and then by boat down the Nile River to Assiout. "When I first saw Assiout," Lillian wrote friends, "I thought it was the most beautiful place in the world."[4] That had to be an optimistic observation from one who had lived in the lush green mountains of western North Carolina.

It did not take her long to be rudely confronted by Egypt's needs: those of the poor, homeless, ragged, rejected children.

After she worked in the mission compound three months, a man knocked on the door one midnight for someone to come and pray with a dying woman. Lillian, accompanied by an interpreter, went, having no idea what she would find. She was horrified to discover a three-month-old girl trying to suck green, stringy milk out of a tin can. Clothes had been sewn tightly on her, and she had not been changed, perhaps since birth. The stench was beyond belief. Lillian prayed and as the mother died she gave the child to Lillian, who took the child back with her to the compound. All night long the two sisters took turns rocking the child and trying to get her to take some milk.

For twelve days and nights they tried, and for twelve days and nights the baby howled. How could such a malnourished child cry so loudly and persistently? Soon, the other missionaries' patience wore out with the two "meddling old maids," and the senior missionary ordered Lillian to take the baby back.

"Back where?" Lillian stuttered.

"Take her back where you found her. The mission work must go on."

Through tears Lillian looked down at tiny Fareida. Lillian had come to Egypt to be a missionary; she had come to work within the traditional mission structure, which insisted that single women be submissive to male leaders. Obviously the veteran missionary knew best.

Back where? ricocheted through her mind. Then the thought struck Lillian and she did not waiver. "I will take her back," she announced.

The senior missionary relaxed.

"But I will go back with her!" she continued.

"Alone?" the superior demanded. "An American woman, unmarried, in an Arab world? Why, you'll be killed or starve to death!"

"Oh, I won't be alone," Lillian responded without hesitation. "I'll have God with me."

With the sixty dollars she had left from her passage money, she rented a small house, and bought a kerosene stove for cooking and some furniture. Although her money was gone (and her mission board support was terminated), she had confidence in God's timing and direction. That day, February 10, 1911, marked the beginning of a new chapter on compassion not only for Lillian Trasher but also for Egypt.[5]

Lillian was truly alone, as her sister returned to Long Beach, California. Years passed before Jenny moved back to Egypt to be at her sister's side. Since she had no missionary support and no government funds, Lillian begged. Her first donation was thirty-five cents, given by a telegraph delivery boy. Not a lot but enough for that day's food.

She traveled on a donkey—the lowest animal in Egyptian society—pleading for money and often receiving children instead. Governmental officials were perplexed that no one "bothered" Miss Lillian. The governor taunted her, "On a donkey? How degrading for a very attractive young lady! A donkey is a symbol of utter debasement, of ridicule."

Lillian interrupted him. "A donkey was good enough for the mother of my Lord. It's certainly good enough for me." Soon the *fellahin* or common people affectionately nicknamed her "Lady on a Donkey."[6]

Day after day, Lillian, compelled by her children's hunger, rode through the deserts, foraging for money or food for her orphans. Despite the heat her children had to eat.

As the orphanage grew, Lillian spent more time wondering about the source of "the next meal." But food or money always arrived.

As her travels carried her farther and farther from the orphanage, she couldn't always get back home at night. If no one offered her a safe place to sleep, she would head for the nearest police station and spend the night with her donkey in a jail cell. Her rugged persistence in the heat won the admiration and financial support of the Egyptian people, who couldn't believe that an American could survive the heat.

By 1914, she had formed a loose affiliation with a new denomination, the Assemblies of God. They sent barrels of clothing and an occasional check but Lillian still relied on the generosity of her Egyptian neighbors.

No matter where it came from, Lillian was grateful for every dollar, and she answered each letter the same day it arrived. "Never let a letter go overnight" was a motto she came to live by.

By 1915, she had fifty children. She added buildings—the children helped with the construction, even making bricks. She added classrooms and began teaching trades; these children must be prepared for life.[7]

By 1923, she housed three hundred orphans and widows but had reaped a dismal spiritual harvest. Not until April 1927 did Lillian witness the revival she had long prayed for. Meanwhile, she survived: sewing, washing, feeding, building.

When the Egyptians rose up against the British rulers, havoc prevailed around Assiout. Lillian relied on God to feed her children, but as the battle lines approached, she decided to move the children from the orphanage to a brick kiln. In the dark of night, with the enemy closing in, she led the children to safety. But once inside the kiln, she counted heads, then recounted. Her heart pounded: two infants were missing.

Against the fervent protests of her fellow workers, she crawled back to the orphanage and found the two terrified toddlers. Tucking a child under each arm, she slowly inched her way back toward the kiln. But suddenly the rebels blocked her path. Her only escape was dropping into a ditch, where she found herself eyeball-to-eyeball with a dead soldier. Knowing that any scream would have brought death to her and her babies, she muffled her horror. The soldiers marched closer and closer, until one of them stepped on Lillian. Apparently assuming that she was dead, he and the others moved on, while Lillian waited, softly singing "Jesus Loves Me" in the ears of the babies. When she felt the danger was over, she crawled to safety with the other staffers and children.[8]

Although nearby houses were looted and burned, the orphanage remained untouched by the terrorists. Lillian knew her God had protected them, and she wasn't shy to tell her Egyptian neighbors of His power.

Slowly she gained the confidence of the Egyptians and of American churches. But when the Great Depression struck, American support money dropped to a trickle. The orphanage, however, continued to grow. Lillian could not turn away hungry children. How do you explain "depression" to small children? she asked. The pressure broke Lillian's heart.

"I can't do this anymore, Lord," she sobbed quietly. "I simply can't!" She wept for several minutes, then quickly knelt beside her chair. "I'll take care of the children, Lord. You provide the money. I can't go out on my donkey anymore to beg. I can't do that and have the strength to care for my children."[9]

The week of that desperate prayer, forty more children arrived on her doorstep. "Which ones do I turn away?" she cried. In those moments of agony she remembered the whispered opinions of the other missionaries, "They'll descend on you in droves!" But Lillian made room for the latest arrivals—every one of them.

There were other heartaches. One of her girls who had been married for ten years returned to Lillian's doorstep with four children. Her husband had gone blind and his family would not keep her and the children. "Of course we took her in," Lillian noted, although it meant five more mouths to feed.[10]

"Can you imagine what it means," she wrote her supporters in 1934, "for me to have the responsibility for seeing that two thousand meals are provided daily as well as books, clothes and the other needs of hundreds of children? This is a heavy job, even if one had all the money needed; it is impossible for us to have enough money for even one day in advance."[11]

When visitors toured the orphanage and found empty cupboards, Lillian explained that she had no bread for the next meal but that she trusted God to supply. Such thinking was difficult for Egyptians and especially for Europeans to accept. Something should be done about such a naive woman!

On her twenty-fifth anniversary in Egypt, a grateful Lillian wrote, "God has never failed me all these years; we are fed like the sparrows which have no barns or storerooms."[12]

Naturally, she sought out wealthy donors to contribute to the financial load. Once she boarded a Nile River steamer and walked the decks asking the Europeans aboard if anyone would like to hear about her orphanage. Crudely, one man blew cigarette smoke in her face.

Another time, Lillian worked frantically to clean and dress the children in order to impress some wealthy European tourists who visited the orphanage. They left, handing her a total of thirteen dollars. Thoroughly frustrated with them, Lillian then invited in an old man who was walking down the street. When he left, he handed her fifty dollars.

"I nearly laughed out loud," she said. "It was such a good lesson to me. I had been working all week to fix up the children and the place for the rich tourists and they gave me thirteen dollars, and a poor old Egyptian whom one scarcely notices hands me a fifty-dollar bill. God's ways are not our ways."[13]

But eventually one of those European tourists did express financial interest. She brought her father, Lord Maclay of Scotland, to visit the orphanage; he gave Lillian one hundred dollars and went home to think about what he'd seen. In February 1935 Lillian received a telegram to come to Cairo at once. There Lord Maclay gave her five thousand dollars. Later, his gifts increased to over twenty thousand dollars and he opened a home for infants in Scotland as well. It was the latter that delighted Lillian. "I was so thrilled to think of those little Scotch babies having a home just because Lord Maclay had seen my work."[14]

After that Santa Claus often looked a lot like a kilt-clad Scot. In February 1937 Lord Maclay and his daughter reappeared and spent the night at the orphanage. When he arrived he gave Lillian two checks: one for twenty-five hundred dollars for the orphanage and another twenty-five hundred dollars for her personal needs. The next morning, however, the lord announced that "the Lord" had spoken to him; then he handed her a check for twenty thousand dollars. Miss Lillian could hardly believe it. What a Christmas and Valentine's gift!

Although some of the financial problems were alleviated, the 1940s presented new problems: war and cholera. When the Germans entered Alexandria, Lillian was urged to flee. Instead she went to prayer to ask the Lord for a promise, which she received. ". . . Fear ye not, stand still, and see the salvation of the Lord, which he will shew to you to day: for the Egyptians whom ye have seen to day, ye shall see them again no more for ever. The Lord shall fight for you, and ye shall hold your peace" (Exodus 14:13, 14). The same Lord who had brought her to Egypt would protect her.

The war also had economic side benefits for the orphanage. As news from the Egyptian front filtered back to the States, Americans were reminded to pray for the orphanage and to send money. Lillian wrote, "Through all the world's suffering and trouble, God has not forgotten the little orphans."[15] When a shipload of American supplies for Greece was diverted to Egypt, the American ambassador offered Lillian part of the goods. Lillian giggled with delight; 2,600 dresses, 1,900 woolen sweaters, blankets, foodstuffs—all for her children.

By autumn 1947, a new terror—worse than the Nazis—faced her: cholera. Lillian knew it would spread like wildfire in the crowded orphanage. She prayed not only that the cholera would not come but that God would take away her fear, the fear she faced every time a new child (a potential carrier) knocked on her door. Although she prayed over each little new one, there was an outbreak but no one died.

A few years later it was the Suez War and Egyptian independence that threatened the orphanage, and the fighting left even more orphans for her to care for. But always—whatever the difficulty or circumstances—there was the prevailing presence of God. In January 1960, she began a new year—her fiftieth in Egypt—with a reflective mood.

"On this day my heart goes back to 1910," she wrote. "I was a young, happy girl of not quite twenty-three, full of dreams of all the wonderful things I was sure life held for me. The most important of all was the twelve children I was hoping for. I wonder what I would have felt like had the curtain been lifted for just a few minutes and I could have seen myself this morning, fifty years later.

"Here I am," she continued, "a tired, old, gray-headed woman—looking out my window and not seeing twelve children but 1,200. I believe the shock would have been more than I could have stood. God, in His wisdom, softly draws the curtain of His love across the future of our lives and lets us live day by day."[16]

What Characterized the Unique Ministry of Lillian Trasher?

Her prayer life. Lillian Trasher's life was bathed in prayer. Even though she begged, she often prayed that God would lead her to the right party. She prayed for flour, for milk, for protection from the terrorists and Nazis, for protection from cholera and polio.

She prayed that Egyptian boys in her orphanage would be called into Christian work; that girls would remain to work in the orphanage; that the Lord would enable her to pay the salaries of her staff on time; that she would be given wisdom and justice; that God would direct her in the decisions set before her. She prayed for strength.

And she taught her children to pray. Several times empty cupboards were replenished when the children prayed. Perhaps her lasting legacy to her children was the gift of prayer and dependency upon God.

Her mercy. Lillian often thought back to that night of great decision. What if she had given in and abandoned the crying baby? What if she had obeyed the older missionary? Or what if the child had not cried for twelve days? The girl would have become "the pet" of the missionaries rather than the impetus for a significant missionary impact on Egypt.

Many people were frustrated, if not annoyed, by Lillian's inability to say no—particularly when she was already overcrowded, and especially during the cholera epidemic.

"People tell me every day," she wrote, " 'Oh, you must not take in any more children; you really must not!' But what can I do? They come, each with their very sad story, and how can I turn them away? Unless our heavenly

Father has changed, He has promised to supply all our needs according to His riches in glory. Will He stop supplying those needs just because I take in a new baby who has just lost its mother? Or because I accept a widow who has just been left with four children? Somehow, I feel that He would do just as I have done—crowd them in and welcome them whether we have room or not."[17]

"Everything would be so easy if there were not quite so many," Lillian noted in March 1952. Meat and candy were in especially short supply. "If a gift of meat comes in *there is seldom enough for everyone.*" Some children had to wait several days for their turn for a meat portion—but God did eventually supply.

Sometimes it wasn't outsiders but friends who challenged Lillian's resolve. One demanded, "Lillian, why do you keep on taking in new children when you have so many needs for the children you already have?" As only a gracious Southerner could, Lillian told her that although she saw her point she couldn't turn anyone away. She made it clear that she never waited for money before she began meeting a need. The only thing she waited for was confirmation of God's will. If He was asking her to do something, she did it. Although the mercy eventually wore down Lillian's health, she never did feel as if she could give enough of it to her children. And maybe that was because of the third characteristic of her ministry.[18]

A sense of being needed. On furlough Lillian once overheard whispers: "Poor Lillian, in that awful summer heat of Assiout with no money and all those children, spending her life in the dirty villages. Oh, what she is missing!"

She laughed. "Poor dears, they don't know what they have missed . . . a chance to make over broken lives and to build up the most wonderful memories a girl can have of her youth. . . . There was the joy of repairing crushed lives, of loving dying babies back to life, of spending my life for God. No, it was not a lost youth. Never! Now the memories are golden, priceless and cannot be taken away."[19]

At age seventy-three, after a brief furlough in the States she hastily returned to her beloved Egypt and then wrote: "No matter how wonderful America is or how wonderfully kind friends are to me, no place in all the world is home to me now but right here with my children. Here *I am needed all day long.*"[20]

Some would think her goal was to get the children raised, married, and out on their own. But there were realities in Egypt; the needs never seemed to diminish.

"Last month I received a telegram that Alfy, who was employed in a government office in Cairo, had suddenly died of a heart attack," she wrote. "I rushed to Cairo for the funeral. It was indeed a very sad time. The children threw their arms around my neck, crying, 'Granny! Granny!' Poor little heart-broken family. Alfy had not been able to leave them anything; even the house rent was in arrears. So I start all over again—just where I began with them twenty-five years ago. They are indeed sad and broken, but their lives will go on the same, if not better."[21]

Of course, Lillian made a place for Alfy's widow and children; seeing the need, she raised a second generation.

In her dying months, Lillian reflected back over the years. "If the Lord allowed me to live my life over, I would do the same thing for another fifty, another hundred years." To those who argued that she had earned a rest, a longer furlough, even retirement, the seventy-three-year-old responded, "As much as I would like to go to heaven and be with Christ, I am not needed there. But these children need me very badly."[22]

A willingness to trust the Lord with results. The missionaries had predicted rape, murder, death, starvation to the strong-willed Lillian as she left the compound with a sick, wailing baby in one arm, a suitcase in the other. But she survived and thrived—as did criticism, which she had to turn over to the Lord.

"I have been told that I have not raised enough preachers and that I have too many children," she reported. "Who knows what God feels about this? It is He who will give the results of the labor. He has followed every step of the orphanage in the past fifty years. It was He who said that a cup of cold water given in His name shall not lose its reward."[23]

On another occasion she wrote supporters: "I wish I were able to give you some wonderful reports to encourage you, but our work is so different from most works. It takes a lifetime for one of my babies to grow up and become important, if ever. . . . Books may be destroyed, papers may be burned or lost, but the seeds planted in the heart of a child may lie dormant for years and then suddenly spring into life."[24]

To charges that she wasn't converting enough Egyptians into Christians, she responded, "Sometimes I get my eyes on results, especially when I read of all those wonderful meetings where thousands are saved and brought to God. Then I begin to wonder if all of the 'glory' really belongs to the preacher. . . . Anyway, our job is planting, and it is God who will give the increase."[25]

After fifty years in the heat of Egypt, Lillian's heart and kidneys were exhausted. Although doctors had prescribed medication, there wasn't always money to buy the medicine. But Lillian had left her mark on Egypt. Now there were grayheaded grandparents whose lives had had a fresh start at the orphanage. Her children had assumed responsible positions in every facet of Egyptian life and society. Hundreds of "Lillians" and "Trashers" were now found in Egyptian schools because alumni named their children after Mama.

By September 9, 1961, Lillian commented, "It is a strange feeling to see oneself slipping away from this life into another." Although she had no fear of death, naturally she wondered, "What will happen to all my children?" Christmas was always a high time at the orphanage with carol singing and the children making presents. But on December 17, 1961, a telegram was received in the Springfield offices of the Assemblies of God: "Mama Lillian died today!"[26]

During fifty years in Egypt, "the Lady on a Donkey" cared for more than eight thousand orphans and widows. The Lillian Trasher Memorial Orphanage thrives today. But an ironic twist exists that only God could have foreseen. God has placed within the Moslem world one nation with a love for Americans. Just miles from its border exists a radical hatred for anything and everything American. It was part of God's good design that Miss Lillian would give her life to be a living model of Jesus Christ in a Moslem world.

She often prayed, "O God, since You have enabled me to do the simple things that I could do, I have full trust in You to do the great things which I cannot do."

Lillian Trasher—one of God's remarkable saints—a single adult who made a difference.

2.

Phillips Brooks

BORN: December 13, 1835

PROFESSION: Minister

DIED: January 23, 1893

In the late 1800s Yale University wrote a young pastor by the name of Brooks, "Among all the inhabitants of the globe you are our first choice. If you cannot bring lectures, bring any of your old sermons."[1] One man, a single adult, changed the way a generation of Americans preached. Although he has been dead almost ninety years, his book on preaching is still widely read and studied.

Popularly, he is known as the writer of "O Little Town of Bethlehem," a traditional part of our Christmas season. Born in 1835 into a distinguished New England family, he had all the advantages of wealth. At age sixteen, the 6-foot-3 Brooks enrolled at Harvard where he divided his notebooks into two parts: facts and ideas from his reading;

reflections on what he had read. Years later as a renowned preacher, he still scrawled notes and ideas for future sermons in his notebooks.

During his days at Harvard he rigorously resisted athletics, and fellow students remember that he exhibited "a profound reserve." Although he had many friends and was greatly admired, few people knew him well. Brooks evaded anyone's curiosity and developed a keen talent for changing the subject when anyone invaded what he considered his "private space." He felt the inner self to be a sacred place to be known only to God.[2]

At age twenty he joined the faculty of the Boston Latin School, but abruptly quit because he could not maintain discipline. He returned to his parents' home, many insist, deeply embarrassed by his failure. Others realize that Brooks was then struggling with a decision unacceptable to many of his fellow Harvard classmates: the ministry.

On the day before he began seminary he scribbled: "As we pass from some experience to some experiment, from a tried to an untried scene of life, it is as when we turn to a new page in a book we have never before read, but whose author we know and love and trust to give us on every page words of counsel and purity and strengthening virtue."[3]

It was a unique time for a Boston Puritan to enter a Virginia seminary—especially a man concerned about the church's attitudes on slavery. Furthermore, the Protestant Episcopal Seminary in Alexandria was a far cry from Harvard. Brooks thought both faculty and facilities poor. The twenty-one-year-old, baffled by Southern attitudes, wrote to his parents, "I feel a little blue; if I wasn't twenty-one years old, I believe, I should say homesick tonight."[4] Brooks considered transferring or even studying at home but chose to remain and graduate.

In 1858, after his graduation, he became rector of the Church of the Advent in Philadelphia. The press covered his first sermon, noting, "Mr. Brooks is quite youthful in his appearance, but evinces talents that are likely to render his services highly acceptable to the people of his prospective charge."[5]

The pastorate suited Brooks, as it was a place to study and to proclaim what was on his mind. Although the death of John Brown deeply influenced Brooks, his father cautioned the young preacher against carrying politics into the pulpit. "Let others trumpet the exploits and virtues of old Brown," he advised. Several years later Brooks admitted that when he preached against slavery he tried to do so "without giving offense."[6] But he always spoke what he felt he must.

Brooks quickly fell into a routine. Mornings he spent reading and preparing sermons. Enthusiastically, he poured himself into study for his two weekly presentations. It was not an easy task, nor did it ever become so, and yet he thrived on it.

Afternoons he visited his parishioners or made sick calls. It was not just the preaching that he felt called to but the pastoring. He loved his people and conscientiously accepted every invitation, every demand, and every request. His pastoral schedule included meetings such as the women's sewing circle, which he attended as an interested observer. He wrote a friend: "You would have been amused to see me (a Harvard man) presiding at the first meeting of my sewing circle the other day, to choose officers, etc. The way women won't be bound by parliamentary rules is very funny."[7]

Brooks was a very sociable being, making friends and seeking out their presence when he was lonely. His biographer, V. G. Allen Alexander, said Brooks had "a hungering for the communion of friendship."[8] Early in his career he enjoyed Sunday evening visits with another rector and occasionally spent the night rather than returning to his lonely home. He often expressed concern about the "whirligig of visiting and sermon-writing" with not even a wedding "to break the monotony."

Brooks's fondness for the company of friends may have been influenced by his strong family ties. He was always saddened when his loyalty to his flock kept him from participating in the traditional family gatherings, such as Thanksgiving. He could "no more go home as a boy to join the family at the dinner table, where the sense of family feeling found its highest expression and sanction." Despite his mother's pleadings and his own sadness, he spent his first holidays in Philadelphia.

Brooks did take some comfort in the fact that his parents were pleased with him. His mother wrote: "Thank you, my dear child, for the joy you have given me in devoting your life to the service of Christ. It was the desire of my heart from your birth, and I gave you up to Him, and I thank Him for accepting my offering. My dear Philly, when I hear of your faithful labors in the ministry, I thank God, and feel that I have not wholly lived in vain."

Mrs. Brooks was always a mother. When he received two calls to more prestigious pulpits she admonished him: "I suppose you feel gratified that you have had those two calls, Philly, but don't let it make you proud. Keep humble like Jesus . . . plead mightily for Christ."[9]

As Mrs. Brooks discovered the talent of her son, she expressed her concern: "I had rather hear you praised for holiness than for talent, though of course that is unspeakably precious when used in God's service. But my dear Philly, let no human praise make you proud but be humble as the Master you serve, and never forget what an honor it is to be a servant of Christ."[10]

As the Civil War loomed on the horizon, Brooks received an invitation to a larger church. He again longed for the carefree security his family had always given him. "I have blue spots every now and then, wishing I was safe at home in the back parlor among the boys and the huckleberries. I can only keep saying 'one of these days' and keep up my spirits."[11]

The invitation was from the governor of Rhode Island who offered Brooks the pastorate of Newport's Trinity Church—at a salary of two thousand dollars and a house. The governor noted that it was "not much of a congregation in the winter" but assured Brooks he would preach to a full house each summer.

As he struggled with his decision, Brooks marveled at the leadership of God in his life. "Doesn't it seem wonderful always to look back on the way that God has led us, and to trace back His guidance ever so far before we began to have any idea that we were under it? How completely it makes us feel that the whole work is in God and not in us, from first to last that He has done it and not we. And how much more satisfied we are that it should be all His doing."[12]

Brooks decided to stay in Philadelphia for the next year—as well as for the Christmas holiday that approached. It was 1860. Lincoln had just been elected and war filled the air. Although he had made plans to spend Christmas Day with a friend, he cancelled everything so that he could preach in his pulpit—in case Jefferson Davis were, by that time, in Philadelphia, "as he might like to attend service at [the

Church of the] Advent and hear what we think of him there. I should have to stay and tell him."[13]

Although Philadelphia was in the North, many Southern sympathizers sat in Brooks's pews. He believed slavery was an anvil on which the courage of the nation and himself would be challenged, and he felt compelled to share his opinions candidly:

"The only restraint was a feeling that I could not speak out as fully as I wished on the one great sin which is beyond doubt the chief reason of this calamity being on us, and which has got to be removed before the calamity can be lifted off. It is useless to talk round and round it, when we know and are sure that slavery, its existence in the South and its approval in the North, is the great crushing, cursing sin of our national life and the cause of all our evils."[14]

Brooks's reputation spread and soon another invitation was extended to him, this time from Holy Trinity, a larger church across Philadelphia. Although he felt the painful hurt of severing his ties with Advent, he accepted the new challenge. The church's repeated inquiries, Brooks felt, had to be an invitation from God and he could not refuse to walk through the open door.[15]

Brooks did not confine his pro-Northern proclamations to the pulpit. On September 27, 1862, he spoke at the Union League, an organization devoted to raising public support for the war. He realized his remarks could alienate some of his wealthier church members. But his persuasive remarks that day caused many to abandon their neutrality and support the Union cause.[16]

And Brooks's political concerns went further than mere words. When the news of the Gettysburg victory reached him, he went to work with the sanitary commission on the battlefield. He distributed clothes, wrote letters for the wounded, and spent time with captured Confederates. He walked through hospital wards, pausing to pray and encourage both armies.

The Emancipation Proclamation set before Brooks yet another cause: to respond to the plight of thousands of free Negroes who were unaccustomed to freedom and now "obliged to seek their own support."[17] In his opinion they were "ignorant, untrained, unfit for the burden placed so suddenly upon them." To help them, Brooks joined the Freedman's Relief Association (again risking the wrath of some of his parishioners); he visited the black troops quartered near Philadelphia and preached to them on Sunday afternoons. It didn't take long for blacks to recognize him as a friend; at social gatherings black waiters often doted on Brooks—much to the chagrin of their employers.

In November 1863, Brooks preached what might be considered his most famous sermon, "Our Mercies of Reoccupation." Chairs were placed in the aisles of Holy Trinity and still people stood along the walls to hear him. The text was from Jeremiah 16:14, 15, which refers to God delivering His people. Brooks blasted his own bishop's attitude toward slavery. He taunted the church's cowardice in opposing slavery; it, rather than the government, should have been the abolition leader.

Brooks launched into an attack on the prejudice that existed in Philadelphia. "Let us get rid of these. If the Negro is a man, and we have freed him in virtue of his manhood, what consistency or honor is it which still objects to his riding down the street in the same car with us if he is tired, or sitting in the same pew with us if he wants to worship God? Brother, the world is not all saved yet. There are a few things still that 'ought not to be.' "[18]

Brooks also questioned the profits that were being made by businessmen. "Every dollar made in these war times ought to be sacred. A man who is making money out of his country's agony must feel like a very Gehazi," referring to Elisha's servant who ran after Naaman and asked the cured leper for money.[19]

Brooks asked his congregation to support the Emancipation Proclamation as wholeheartedly as they had the Declaration of Independence. The sermon was printed and distributed across the nation and stirred a national debate.

Eighteen months later, on Good Friday, Brooks learned of Lincoln's assassination. Although he had a triumphal sermon prepared, he decided not to preach at all on Easter. But once he was at the church presiding over the service, he felt compelled to speak without notes.

"If ever our whole hearts and thoughts ought to be in the spirit of Easter, it is this Easter above all; for Easter celebrates the glorious victory through Christ of humanity over the grave; . . . when death had dealt to us a most tremendous blow, do we not need the Easter Day of all days? . . .

"We are met today not to eulogize the dead," he continued, "but simply to pour out our tears before the living God in company with the living. We are not as those who meet in an assemblage to praise some great man of the world. We are met like children who gather round the hearthstone the night their father dies to tell one another how much they loved him, and how they mourn his loss."[20]

The next afternoon, he addressed the women of Philadelphia: "God allowed Abraham Lincoln to stay until he stood at the grave of slavery. God allowed him to stand

and look on the land and not see a black face which was not radiant with freedom. Slavery had been blotted out before God called him to his rest."[21]

While such remarks naturally drew applause, Brooks used the occasion to attack an area of his concerns: "the frivolities and extravagances" of Philadelphians.

When the war ended, Philadelphia returned to its normal life, and Brooks's life was a little less intense. Although his knowledge of music was limited, Phillips Brooks took great delight in the art, even the singing of his Sunday school children, and he did not hesitate to state his opinions on music. Lewis Redner, his organist at Holy Trinity, recalled that Brooks wasn't "much of a singer but when a strain of music pleased him it impressed him so that he was constantly singing it."[22]

Brooks attended music committee meetings at Redner's house—spending the hours in a big, comfortable chair reading. If he heard a tune he liked, he called out, "I like that!" He liked simple music, and music was especially important to him on his lengthy trip to Palestine. Redner had given him a hymnal which he carried with him as he walked the walls of Jerusalem singing "God Rest Ye, Merry Gentlemen" to Redner's tune.

For Christmas 1868, Brooks wrote a poem inspired by the months he'd spent in Palestine. Redner composed the tune, and it immediately became popular.

> *O little town of Bethlehem*
> *How still we see thee lie!*
> *Above thy deep and dreamless sleep*
> *The silent stars go by.*
> *Yet in thy dark streets shineth*

The everlasting Light;
The hopes and fears of all the years
Are met in thee tonight.

For Christ is born of Mary,
And gathered all above,
While mortals sleep, the angels keep
Their watch of wondering love.
O morning stars, together
Proclaim the holy birth!
And praises sing to God the King,
And peace to men on earth.

How silently, how silently,
The wondrous gift is given!
So God imparts to human hearts
The blessings of His heaven.
No ear may hear His coming
But in this world of sin,
Where meek souls will receive Him still,
The dear Christ enters in.

O holy child of Bethlehem!
Descend to us, we pray;
Cast out our sin, and enter in;
Be born in us today.
We hear the Christmas angels
The great glad tidings tell;
O come to us, Abide with us,
Our Lord Emmanuel.

The fifth verse, however, is seldom sung:

> *Where children pure and happy*
> *Pray to the blessed Child*
> *Where misery cries out to Thee*
> *Son of the Mother mild.*
> *Where charity stands watching*
> *And faith holds wide the door,*
> *The dark night wakes, the glory breaks*
> *and Christmas comes once more.*

As Brooks's fame as a pulpiteer spread across the nation, visitors to Philadelphia included a visit to Holy Trinity on Sundays. His reputation and books of sermons led to a call to Boston's prestigious Trinity Church, which he accepted. When he resigned in July 1869, an incredible outcry rose from the city of Philadelphia—not only from the mighty and pious but also from the common people. One young mother who had lost her only child remarked, "He is the one person who has seemed to me to enter into my grief as if he really shared it."[23]

Brooks had not been in Boston long before fire destroyed Trinity Church. He then preached to two packed audiences in nearby Huntington Hall and devoted many hours to a new responsibility—supervising the architectural plans for a new sanctuary. He insisted that big balconies be designed, as all pews on the main floor were "taxed," not "free."[24]

In time, Phillips Brooks became Boston's preacher—not just the rector of the massive edifice on Copley Square. Rich and poor alike considered him their friend.

His singleness had a decisive impact on his success: he was always available. In Boston, his schedule for a typical day began at 7:00 A.M. when he awakened singing. After breakfast at 8:00, he studied in the morning and received callers, "refusing no one." In the afternoons, he called on the sick and attended meetings. He had dinner at six, then more calling or often preaching in other churches. When he returned he usually found people waiting for him. He went to bed at eleven.

One guest who stayed in the parsonage calculated that the doorbell rang, on the average, every five minutes. He did not know social class. After being away and receiving his mail, he accepted social invitations in the order he opened them.[25]

On one occasion he was to meet friends at his manse at 8:00 P.M. to attend a reception. Brooks arrived three hours late, explaining that he had been at the hospital with a black man who had sent for him. "But why did *you* have to go?" one friend needled him. "Why didn't you send an assistant?"

Because, Brooks explained, "the man had sent for me."[26]

Although he was consumed with the lives of his parishioners, he regretted not marrying. His biographer noted that he sometimes seemed to covet the familial happiness of his youngest friends. Brooks once scolded some men, "The trouble with you married men is that you think no one has been in love but yourselves."

He relied heavily on friends and dreaded returning to a quiet house where no one welcomed him. Yet, he did not moan and groan over his celibacy but forced himself to discover the brighter side.[27]

One good thing about life in Boston—Brooks was closer to his family, which was so important to him.

Often he went to his brother's home in Boston on Sunday night after church and listened to his nephews recite poetry. He took his nieces and nephews shopping for their Christmas presents and then asked them to forget what they had selected. And no presents could be opened on Christmas until "Uncle Phillips" arrived and that after Christmas services. But they, "his children," waited patiently.

Brooks's mother always maintained her strong influence over him. Till her dying day she demanded strict Sabbath observance from her sons. Once when she thought there was too much noise, she stuck her head into the room and admonished her grown sons, "Boys, remember it is Sunday!" And the boys complied.

When Brooks was on the steamer returning to America after having preached to Queen Victoria, someone asked him if he hadn't found it difficult to preach before the queen.

"Not at all," he replied. "You see, I have often preached before my mother."[28]

When his parents grew older, Brooks invited them to live with him and when his mother died, he was devastated. "I did not know," he confessed, "I could ever be so much like a child again; tonight the world seems very desolate and lonely." He missed his mother deeply. "Now that she is with God, I seem to know for the first time how pure and true and self-sacrificing all her earthly life has been."[29]

Brooks had yet other demands on his time. Parents from across the country sent letters to him asking him to check up on students attending college in Boston. He complied and took a particular interest in Harvard students, frequently preaching in chapel. In 1881, he was offered a professorship in Christian ethics and the post of university "preacher." He reluctantly declined both posts and the chaplaincy was abolished. Soon thereafter, compulsory chapel was also abolished because Brooks, a trustee, supported the measure. He reasoned that forcing Harvard men to attend chapel did not make them into saints; rather the power of preaching should draw them to chapel. One wonders what Harvard would be like today if Brooks had accepted that post.

As he grew older, Brooks's preaching and teaching of homiletics were acknowledged around the world. After declining the office of assistant bishop, preferring the task of preaching, he was, on April 29, 1891, elected bishop by a large majority despite charges that his doctrine was unsound. Although he did not respond to the charges, he admitted that his communion table had been open to all Christians, which was then not the practice of the Episcopal Church.[30]

Finally, after much debating and ecclesiastical wrangling, he was consecrated. Holy Trinity was packed for the great ceremony that honored such a great man who urged his students—and us—to reach beyond our own abilities:

"Do not pray for easy lives. Do not pray for tasks equal to your powers. Pray for power equal to your tasks. If the life you have chosen to be your life is really worthy of you, it involves self-sacrifice and pain. If your Jerusalem is your sacred city, there is certainly a cross in it. Ask God to fill you with Himself, and then calmly look up and go on. Disappointment, mortification, misconception, enmity, pain, death—these may come to you, but if they come to you in doing your duty it is all right."[31]

What Characterized the Unique Ministry of Phillips Brooks?

His message. In his famous lectures at Yale in 1877, he asked, "What is preaching?" Then he answered, "Preaching is the communication of truth by man to men."

Preaching has two essential elements: truth and personality, neither of which can be spared. "Preaching is the bringing of truth through personality," he said.[32]

Brooks's message was that he "preached Christ." He explained, "That old phrase, which has been the very watchword of cant, how it still declares the true nature of Christian teaching. Not Christianity but Christ. Not a doctrine but a person. Christianity only for Christ."[33]

He avoided doctrinal issues. "Make known and real to men by every means you can command the personal Christ, not doctrine about Him, but Him!"[34]

Naturally, there were those who attempted to imitate Brooks's style. One young man wrote to ask the secret of his life. Brooks, who personally answered all his correspondence in longhand, mused over the answer for some time before he responded that the secret was "a deeper knowledge and truer love of Christ. . . . I cannot tell you how personal this grows to me. He is here. He knows me and I know Him. It is no figure of speech. It is the realest [sic] thing in the world. And every day makes it realer, and one wonders with delight what it will grow to as the years go on."[35]

Yet Phillips cautioned, "Never dare to say in the pulpit or in private, through ardent excitement or conformity to what you know you are expected to say, one word which at the moment when you say it, you do not believe."[36] Honesty was essential in preaching and living the Christian life. His favorite text was, ". . . I am come that they might have life, and that they might have it more abundantly" (John 10:10). Nothing could take the place of knowing Christ who gave the abundant life.

His pulpit persona. Admittedly, his personality "filled" the pulpit. In his prime, weighing three hundred pounds and standing 6-foot-4, he conducted himself with dignity. Justice Harlan of the U.S. Supreme Court described him as "the most beautiful man I have ever seen." Although Brooks began a sermon softly, he gained momentum until he averaged 200 words per minute with the effect of "an express train rushing through a station."[37] Foreign clerics and theologians who came to critique him were overwhelmed.

Brooks also identified with his audience; he was a good listener. James Bryce studied Brooks's preaching style and said, "He spoke to his audience as a man might speak to his friend, pouring out with swift, yet quiet and seldom impassioned earnestness . . . the listeners never thought of style or manner, but only of the substance of his thoughts. They were entranced and carried out of themselves by the strength and sweetness and beauty of the aspects of religious truth and its helpfulness to weak human nature which he presented."[38]

His love of people and his servanthood. Brooks lived out his servanthood. So devoted was he to his members that leaving each of the three charges (Advent, Holy Trinity, Trinity of Boston) was agonizing for him. When he resigned to become bishop he wrote, "In giving up Trinity Church, I know what it must be to die."[39]

Brooks had the gift of inspiring depressed people. With "one word from him they returned to their tasks with renewed energy" and it wasn't just his members who sought his counsel. He was pastor to all Boston. The balconies were packed with the poor, the rejected. One man wrote that although he was not a member or a

Christian, he "felt my life was immensely better and richer because I lived in the same city as Phillips Brooks."[40]

Helen Keller once said that she had always known there was a God "but had not known his name" until she met Brooks.[41] Brooks invested a lot of time with theology students at Boston University, Andover, and Harvard Divinity School. That investment of time shaped ministry for decades to come.

But how did Brooks find time to prepare to preach so brilliantly and still work with people?

His belief in the dignity of all human beings. Many who have carefully studied his writing and preaching find the forerunning of possibility thinking. His study of New England had convinced him of what he labeled the dangers of "endless discussion of fanatical questions" and the "minute and morbid study of their spiritual conditions." Brooks was concerned with what he termed "the arrested spiritual development of that intense religious life" that "wrought its inevitable consequences." Brooks argued, instead, that "men are nobler than they think themselves to be. There is in every man something greater than he has begun to dream of. When he gives himself to Jesus Christ in consecration, then it begins to come forth. Break through the cross of your despair and ask Christ to let you see yourself as He sees you, all stained with sin but with the divine image in you all the time."[42]

He found people fascinating and said, "I believe fully that the intrinsic life of any human being is so interesting that if it can be simply and sympathetically put into words, it will be legitimately interesting to other men."[43]

Brooks admitted, "I would rather have written a great biography than a great book of any sort, and I would rather have painted a great portrait than any other kind of picture." He explained that, after all, the Bible wasn't based on doctrine but on biography. His personal views of God and his neighbors permeated everything he did.[44]

His sense of humor. The sight and sound of a three-hundred-pound man laughing spontaneously encouraged others to follow his example. When one skeptic challenged the feasibility of the story of Jonah, Brooks explained that Jonah could have been swallowed because he was a "minor" prophet.

When some self-righteous people demanded to know why some atheists lived such moral lives, Brooks quipped, "They have to; they have no God to forgive them if they don't."[45]

Even his mannerisms could prompt laughter. Whenever he traveled, he read intensely; Brooks was never distracted but he would cause some commotion himself when he promptly tossed a finished book out the window.

The three-hundred-pound pastor loved to play Goliath with small boys with sling shots, and children were delighted when he lit his cigar from street lamps.

Eighteen months after he was elected bishop, Brooks died—on January 23, 1893. He did not fear death. On one birthday he scribbled, "Let us hope the rest of our time, till we are 58 or 60, will go as smoothly as the past, and then we can say good-bye to the world as to a very kind old friend.[46]

"Surely," he wrote, "with all these that have gone before, it will not be hard to go to Him when our time comes."[47]

All of Boston mourned his death. Trinity Church was again packed for the memorial service, and a second service had to be conducted outdoors for the thousands who could not get in. His body was taken to Harvard and carried on the shoulders of students across campus. Some ninety-five thousand dollars were contributed spontaneously for a memorial.

Today, in Trinity Church, Boston, one can find the statue of Brooks done by Augustus Saint-Gaudens. Brooks stands in his pulpit and Christ stands behind him, His hand resting on Brooks's shoulder.

His legacy cannot be forgotten. His sermons challenged the conscience of a nation, and his singleness provided the season for greatness.

"And how shall we gain nearness to God and power?" he asked. "You never become truly spiritual by sitting down and wishing to become so. You must undertake something so great that you cannot accomplish it unaided. Begin doing something for your fellow men and if you do it with all your power, it will almost immediately bring you face to face with problems you cannot solve: you need God and you need to go to God."[48]

3.

Belle Bennett

BORN: December 3, 1852

PROFESSION: Christian educator

DIED: July 20, 1922

"I'll do it!" Belle said in the middle of the night, wakening from her dream. Three years had passed since her conversion, and this dream seemed like signing a blank check—giving God anything He desired. Later, she explained, "Almost without knowing what I did, I responded to the urgings of His Spirit."[1]

That "I'll do it" eventually meant founding a great college, significantly influencing the professional training of missionaries, attaining full rights for women in the Methodist Church, and a host of other achievements. Many of the rights and privileges women take for granted today were earned through the efforts of Belle Bennett.

Her biographer, J. L. Cuninggim, wrote: "I would rather

have been that woman, with all the deeds of such a wonderfully useful life following me into eternity, than to have been a queen on any throne, in any empire or kingdom, and in any age of the history of the world."[2]

Belle was born into a prosperous politician's home, near Richmond, Kentucky, on December 3, 1852. All seven of the children born to Samuel and Elizabeth Bennett were high achievers: one became a physician, one a state senator, and one a lawyer, and two of the daughters founded colleges.

The family attended a Methodist church built on land owned by Belle's father, and every Sunday afternoon visitors were invited home for dinner at the big colonial house; as many as thirty people crowded in and enjoyed Southern hospitality around the big dining room table.

Because of the family's economic and political status, Belle was sent to the best schools. In Richmond, she attended a private school taught by Robert Breck, a noted classical scholar. Then she went to a boarding school in Nazareth and later to an elite school for young "Western" women—in College Hill, Ohio. Belle, a gifted musician who loved art and drama, often traveled to Louisville to attend concerts and the theatre.

Obviously her education was designed to prepare Belle for high social standing, but her natural beauty—her blue eyes, ash blonde hair, and creamy complexion—her poise, and her articulate charm were the characteristics that made her the talk of central Kentucky. She spent two social seasons in Frankfort, the state capital, as a guest of her brother, Senator John Bennett. She turned heads at social functions, was described as "the gayest of the gay," and was a reigning belle for several years at the New Orleans Mardi Gras.[3]

But despite the courters, she never found a charming "prince" she was willing to marry.

It's clear that God had other plans for Belle. Although she joined a small Methodist church at age 22, when she was 31, she attended a Presbyterian revival and "caught a vision" of a kingdom won by Christ and of persons like herself working with Him. Seeing this as God's eternal purpose for the universe, Belle committed herself fully to Christ and to service through the church.[4]

But first she had to tend to family responsibilities. When her brother William died, leaving four children, Belle and her sister Sue, also unmarried, cared for them. When her father died, the family moved from their country home into Richmond. Only a year later Belle was devastated when Sue also passed away. She lost a great friend and also had to assume more responsibility for her aging mother and the family's social obligations.

For Belle, becoming more active in the church was synonymous with taking on leadership roles. By 1888, she was president of the Kentucky Conference Women's Society. From that position she clearly saw a disturbing practice of the denomination.[5]

The Methodists had begun sending out single women as foreign missionaries; the controversial practice fostered a spirit of independence that married missionaries found objectionable. But that wasn't what bothered Belle. These women simply weren't adequately trained for the work they were sent to do. She asked how young women, particularly single, although "consecrated and courageous" could bring "good news" to a foreign country without knowing the language and without skills in health and social practices. Admittedly women had access to women in foreign countries where husbands were suspicious of American male missionaries, but Belle was not satisfied. As a member of the Committee on Examination of Missionary Candidates, the procedures troubled her:

[One young woman] who was a volunteer for appoint-ment that year . . . met us in St. Louis and we pro-ceeded to question her. My own part of the examination consisted of asking how much she knew about the Bible, how she had learned it and how she expected to teach it to people who had a religion of their own. She said she didn't know anything much. She was a district school teacher and had always at-tended Sunday school, and had heard of the wretched conditions of the women in heathen lands.[6]

Such answers were too much for Belle. There must be a place where such candidates could be "taught" to become missionaries. If ministers went to seminaries, musicians to conservatories, doctors to medical schools, why not have a missionary-training school?

When she asked who would start such a school, she remembered her vision and her answer, "I'll do it." In the 1870s a Southern revival had rekindled missionary zeal, and Belle knew that church women were looking for something in which to invest their lives. If young women went to the mission field, surely married women at home could support them. Besides, Belle reasoned, reading about missions and working in missionary societies would stretch the minds of young matrons. Any excuse that they were "too busy" with homemaking responsibilities was gently but effectively rebuffed.

The first efforts to found a national women's missionary organization in the Methodist Episcopal Church, South, were rejected by the church's male hierarchy. So the society slowly took root at the grass levels, prompted by concerned women like Belle. A meeting of the organization in 1889, in Little Rock, Arkansas, changed the direction of Methodist history—as well as the life of Belle Bennett.

Belle had shared her concept of a missionary training school with many people. But the president of the women's society, Mrs. Juliana Hayes, wanted more than polite conversation over tea. She asked Belle to speak to the meeting. Belle was terrified.

"I was too sick and frightened to stand on my feet when I was called to speak before the board. The president, seeing my condition, rose out of her chair and said, 'Come right here, Miss Bennett, sit down in this chair, and talk it over with us.'

"I did it, but then I stood up when I became excited! I poured out the whole thought of my heart. I talked to them about the splendid training that was being given to doctors and lawyers and professional men of all kinds. Yet we were trying to send out young women to the great dark lands to teach a new religion that they themselves knew nothing about."[7]

She finished, and silence prevailed in the room. Then someone suggested that they ask God to send the Methodists such a school for women missionaries. The prayer was hardly finished when a resolution was passed: to present the needs to the entire Methodist Church. Belle, in a state of mild shock, was appointed to travel across the land to raise money for the project.

Because of her family obligations she hesitated until she remembered her vow, "I'll do it." Churches and parsonages opened to her—although not always to her ideas.

The first dollar she collected she received in the home of Dr. William Thompson. His adopted daughter gave Belle a silver dollar she had earned while waiting on tables. Later, Mary McClellan, after hearing a stirring missionary address, contributed a note in the offering: "I give five dollars and myself."[8]

It wasn't long before one of the more vocal Methodist bishops indignantly demanded, "Who is this Belle Bennett anyway? By what authority is she going through the church collecting money?"

Those words and the attitude behind them won Belle the support of prominent Southern evangelist Samuel Porter Jones, who had little love for the bishops. If the bishops were giving Belle problems (as they were him), she was his natural ally. And besides, Jones's wife had been raised near Richmond and had a warm spot for Kentuckians.

Jones, excited about the plans for the school, invited Belle to attend his great camp meetings and donated the offerings from one service per encampment to the school. Sometimes, he started the pledges himself. Once he pledged five hundred dollars for his wife and "forgot to pay" until Belle wrote him and urged him to "pay up." In one such meeting in Mississippi, Belle received three thousand dollars—a sizable sum in those days.[9]

Thus, the little girl's silver dollar became a leaven. On one train trip to Kansas City, Belle shared her dream with a stranger. Touched by what he heard, the man mailed Belle a check for one thousand dollars. At the end of the first year of the campaign she reported, "Untried and unknown I was sent out as directed in God's strength . . . and I return to report the great things which He has done. From the day I received my commission at your hands, to this time, wherever I have gone, men, women, children have responded. From the old and young and rich and poor, donations have come—some with streaming eyes, and many with a fervent 'God bless you!' Women have taken earrings from their ears and watches from their bosoms, saying, 'Take these. We have no money but we want to give something!' "[10]

The question was no longer "should?" but "where?" And that question was answered when Dr. Nathan Scarritt offered land in Kansas City, Missouri, worth $25,000, and he pledged a matching $25,000 if the school would be located there. Although Kansas City was a long way from her beloved South, Belle knew that such a commitment by a man would engender even more support from the hostile male hierarchy of the Methodist Episcopal Church, South.

A hitch developed, however, when Dr. Scarritt made it clear that he wanted to prepare home missionaries as well as foreign. The resolution under which Belle was authorized to collect funds had read, "To enlist and unite the efforts of men and women and children in sending the gospel to the women and children of *heathen* countries." Belle wanted to agree to Scarritt's stipulation but was strongly opposed by the general secretary of the Women's Board of Foreign Missions. In the process, Belle learned a valuable lesson about church politics.

Belle discovered a precedent and built a case. Had not the church authorized missions in Mexico? Mexico certainly was not "heathen" nor were the American Indians who also received funds from the Foreign Missionary Board. Slowly her opposition relented and in May 1890, the way was paved for what became the Scarritt Bible and Training School, now Scarritt College. A board of managers was appointed with Belle as vice president; ground was broken for the first building on April 28, 1891.

Now that the school had been established and a building started, Belle immersed herself in planning the curriculum for the young women. They had to learn more than theology and evangelism. Belle wanted biblical training with hands-on practical experience. Nurses' training must also be offered. Belle went to Kaiserworth, Germany, to study the deaconess movement, a move within the Methodist Church to give recognition to the growing numbers of women who wanted to be involved in ministry, yet had no desire to be ordained to preach the gospel. This gave "official" status to women doing what the male hierarchy labeled "women's work." She interviewed missionary wives, and asked them to describe what was needed of their fields.

About this time, some two hundred women in Shanghai addressed a letter "to the Christian Women of the British Empire, the United States, Germany and other Protestant Countries." This extraordinary letter identified four areas of work open to women missionaries and suggested the qualifications for such work:

1. There is school work in connection with our various missions which in many cases the men have handed over to the women, in order that they themselves may be free to engage more directly in evangelistic work.

2. There is work to be done for the sick and the suffering in hospitals, dispensaries and homes. Most of the work can be better done by women than by men, and much of it can only be done by women.

3. There is work for us in the families of the church.

There are mothers and daughters who need to be taught the way of the Lord more perfectly.

4. There is work of evangelization among women. . . . There is much of it that men cannot do as well as women.

Belle was delighted with the letter, as it strengthened her position—that missionary candidates must be properly qualified. The letter continued:

1. They should be women of sound health, of good ability, and of good common sense, also well-educated, though not necessarily of the highest education—apt to teach, kind and forbearing in disposition, so that they may live harmoniously with their associates, and win the hearts of the Chinese.

2. Above all they should be women who have given themselves wholly to the Lord's work—and are prepared to bear hardship and exercise constant self-control for Christ's sake.

3. It is desirable that they should pursue a systematic course in Bible study before coming to China and that they have had some experience in Christian work at home.[11]

The letter of another missionary, Laura Haygood of Shanghai, addressed to Bishop Hendrix, the chairman of the board of managers of the school, was also helpful. Haygood suggested that missionaries needed to know about other religions and have an understanding for the cultures in which they would live. This sounded a lot like anthropology, a program taught in few schools in that day.

With a firm direction for curriculum, the board elected Belle the first president (or principal), but she declined, not wanting the fund-raising responsibilities she knew the position would entail. Besides, a man would probably raise more money than a woman—and there were other aspects of the vision of God's kingdom that she wanted to explore. Scarritt—Belle Bennett's dream child—opened on September 14, 1892.

Belle tackled race relations next; her sensitivities were decades ahead of the times, especially for a Southerner. People had heard about China, Japan, and India. They prayed for doors to open in Africa. But Belle wanted to know why the church wasn't doing something for Africa at home.[12]

Belle had been raised in the South; she remembered the Civil War and Reconstruction. She knew firsthand the hatred and racial prejudice. Yet she dared suggest to a pastor's conference that the race problem would be solved if Southern Methodist preachers had the courage of the apostle Paul who said, "Neither count I my life dear unto myself" (Acts 20:24). Obedience, "the cost of fellowship with God," drove Belle to speak out on the subject.

"If you men who stand in the pulpits with honest and sincere hearts say to your congregations, 'These black-faced, ignorant child peoples are *my* brothers and sisters and I intend to treat them as such,' the Negro problem would soon be solved."[13]

Knowing that racial prejudice would be slow to die out, Belle not only preached good race relations, she lived it. She loaned one local black congregation $4,000, and in the next fifteen years that church paid her back, bringing small payments tied up in handkerchiefs and stockings. Whenever blacks needed money, Belle lent it to them.

But money wasn't the only answer for the Africa that was "nearer than home." One day Belle called a black pastor and asked what she could do to help. "Miss Belle," he laughed, "I've been praying for nearly a year that you might spare us some of your time, but you seemed so busy." She invited him to come and see her and they drew up plans for a Bible study which eventually drew three hundred to four hundred black people in Richmond.[14]

Belle's mission was larger than social "do-gooding." One's first commitment, she thought, was to love, and she saw that the impetus for love had to be based on spiritual discipline. She committed a great deal of her own time to prayer and Bible study, but she also encouraged others to do likewise.

"Oh, how we need the quiet times to let God speak to us. You, His leaders, need far more than any of those around you the quiet hour when God may speak to you. Each day is full of work for God's chosen ones, but prayer is the work of God's chosen ones; prayer is the greatest part of each day's work."[15]

Belle Bennett testified to a prayer-answering God. "Intercession," she wrote, "is the greatest fruit-bearing work that God gives us to do."[16]

As you can imagine, she received a volume of correspondence, and she was known to bow her head and pray for wisdom when answering particularly difficult letters. No matter was too small to be prayed over. To her friends she wrote, "I do not fail to pray for you more and oftener than I can say." She prayed for them and equally for her enemies and critics. It was a habit that she learned early in life and which held her in good stead when the church turned against her and her ideas.

Belle committed chapters and whole books to memory and claimed to be most happy when she was studying her Bible with friends. She discovered "that to study His Word with someone and get His will together in prayer strengthens me more than I can say."[17]

Bible awareness became a torch Belle carried among the missionary candidates and among the women of the church in general. She was convinced that the moral teachings of the Bible were fundamental to personal and national character. Publicly to large audiences and privately in personal conversation, she continually encouraged people to earnest, intelligent Bible study periods. Her biographer, Mrs. R. W. MacDonell, attributed Belle's leadership success to her Bible study and prayer: "The knowledge that God had placed her in leadership sent her to earnest and diligent study of the Bible."[18]

Mrs. MacDonell also wrote, "She was never argumentative in presenting what she believed the Word of God taught; she had a way of assuming the concurrence of her hearers with such persuasive power that she impelled assent," yet Belle urged that her students be cautious and wise in teaching young people and new believers who would easily accept a teacher's word as the gospel truth.

As important as her Bible study was to her, it led her to a startling discovery that gave her yet another battle to fight. Belle's most important contribution was probably to the rights of women in the church, yet the issue was her personal Gethsemane.

Belle's constant appeal to Methodist women was to "keep up the morals of the Christian home and spiritual life of the church that the nation might not lose its highest values." She was accepted when she preached "women's work for women," but when she started rattling the cages about the place of women in the church, she ran into opposition. The bureaucracies in the Methodist Episcopal Church, South, naturally led to frustration: No woman could serve as a delegate or even speak at the general conference. Any decision of the women's missionary society had to be ratified "by the men" of Methodism.

In one sense the very success—in building up the women's missionary organization—contributed to her problems. The women took more of an interest in church affairs and wanted more control of their efforts.

"Would the women be content until they are in the pulpit?" some ministers demanded. Some saw the budding deaconess work as a viable channel for the women's energy. One bishop urged fellow ministers to ignore the women's movement, assuring them that it would die out. A debate ensued and then turned sour. Eventually women were ridiculed, censured, and scoffed at.

Up to this point, the words "laity" and "laymen" referred to males; but Belle Bennett didn't understand Scripture to undergird such a position. She was encouraged in her position when Frances Willard and four other women were elected delegates to the general conference of the Methodist Episcopal Church, North, although they were barred from taking their seats.

By 1906, Belle was declaring enthusiastically, "Both men and women were created in God's image and to both God came in the flesh of Jesus Christ."

Further, "the so-called worldwide movement for the liberation and uplift of women is distinctly and insistently the result of the teachings of Jesus Christ and the operation of the Holy Spirit upon the hearts of men. From the time when its divine Founder rebuked in scathing terms the teachings of the scribes, Pharisees and hypocrites in

Judaism, the dominant note in Christianity, even in its lowest forms, has been a note of liberty. A Christian civilization which does not generate and develop a spirit of individual, civil and religious liberty is impossible."[19]

Her detractors were caught in a bind: Belle's spirituality and her skilled use of Scripture gained recognition and threatened those who held to their male-dominated positions.

Remember, this debate took place concurrently with the fight over national suffrage for women. Prior to 1909, Belle Bennett was the most highly respected woman in the Southern Methodist Church. Informally she was consulted about the most important church business. When Belle spoke, church officials listened. But slowly the brunt of the criticism about the women's issue turned to Belle herself.

In 1910, Belle, the woman who had represented the denomination at the Ecumenical Methodist Conference in London in 1901 and the World Missionary Conference in Edinburgh, rose to the platform to speak to the general conference on the subject of laity rights. Her voice was the first woman's voice ever heard at the highest gathering of Methodists, but her words were not well received; her invitation to speak on missions at the Fourth Ecumenical Methodist Conference in Toronto was rescinded. Belle struggled with her hurt and her despondency. Nevertheless, she knew she had two commitments: to continue to work to gain equality for women and to respond to the personal attacks with kindness. She always debated the issue of women's role and rights; she did not deal with the character of those who opposed her point of view.[20]

Keeping a motto in front of her: "Obedience is the key that unlocks the treasure house of God," she continued her fight. When the first memorial for lay rights for women was voted down, the women regrouped. In the

1914 general conference, women on both sides of the issue debated; although the issue was again defeated, the margin of opposition had been reduced. Belle realized that growing global influences (a war in Europe and the involvement of women in defense industries and the war effort) would eventually have an effect on the church. Besides, if the world moved to enfranchise women, how could the church do less?

In 1918, the subject again was debated by the general conference; this time the outcome looked hopeful—that women would be given full participation in the conference. After the vote was announced—265 for, 57 against— the male delegates rose from their seats, bowed and waved to the women, watching from the galleries. As a group, the women stood and bowed back.[21]

Belle was delighted, but she knew the church hierarchy too well to celebrate prematurely. She wanted no congratulations for the honor, saying, "Don't, women! Don't congratulate me. We are not so foolish as to count the battle won!" The various regional annual conferences, "where the greater struggle must begin," were before the women, as it was there that the momentous action of the general conference would really be implemented.[22]

Four years later, Belle was an elected delegate, but she was conspicuously absent. Her fight against cancer was taking a toll on her and she was too ill to attend. W. F. Tillett, a long-time dean of Vanderbilt Divinity School and her friend, wrote to her: "It is a source of profound regret to your many friends throughout the church that after leading the women of Southern Methodism to the promised land of membership in the general conference you could not be present on the opening day of general conference to enter with those of your sisters who had been elected like yourself to this high honor and important service."[23]

Belle Bennett was tired after long service "at the altars of her church." For thirty-five years she had worked without any financial compensation; the work had grown tremendously, but her health had been worn down.

The long battle was nearly over. She recalled all the conversations on women's spheres or women's work. She wisely penned, "There is but one inflexible sphere—the sphere of old age which God in mercy breaks with the hammer of death." Belle perceived death to be only another chapter, another episode in her life. Two days before her death, she cried, "I wish the Master would come for me; I am so tired, so tired of waiting."

And He did—on July 20, 1922, Belle Bennett was taken home.

What Characterized the Unique Ministry of Belle Bennett?

Belle ranks as one of the greatest women of all American Methodism. Obviously, she used her singleness to impact the world. What contributed to this woman's success?

Her financial resourcefulness. Carolyn Stapleton explains that by "virtue of her family's wealth, she had no worries in regard to her own financial needs." There is no indication that she was ever paid for her efforts. For example, in 1919, when she and Mrs. Luke Johnson toured war-torn Europe to determine how the church could assist recovery, not even her expenses were reimbursed.[24]

Eventually she gave up her Richmond home and moved into a hotel to have more time to devote to church work and less to housekeeping. When she traveled for long stints, she locked everything of value in the closet and permitted the hotel manager to rent out the room while she was gone. When someone questioned her about the habit, she explained quickly that in one year the income paid in room rent during her absences would finance a year of college for some deserving man or woman.[25]

In fact, some were concerned about her generosity. "To give was the first requisite of her nature," one friend quipped, yet Belle did not shrink from family responsibilities. When her brother became ill, she personally nursed him for two years although she could have hired professionals.

Her concern for other people's children. Belle once said, "I never married, never had children of the flesh, but God has given me many spiritual children."[26] She often had as many as eight or ten of her nieces and nephews as her guests at the hotel. When in New York, she entertained her nieces who were Vassar College students.

She was concerned about unwed mothers and supported the Virginia Johnson Home in Dallas. She also called attention to "fallen men" and pleaded for a high but single standard of morality. She lobbied for wives of sailors and soldiers during World War I; she sought their admission as special students in colleges and lobbied for the colleges to provide free baby-sitting.[27]

Her friendship and graciousness. Belle spent a great deal of effort nurturing personal relationships and endearing people to her. She did not remember unkindnesses.

She took note of events to celebrate: a birth, a young girl's graduation, a wedding. She worked hard to select gifts that would have a special meaning to the recipient. She sent so many Christmas presents that her friends wondered where she ever found the time to buy and wrap them. When she was on the road, she always sent postcards.[28]

Naturally, there were those times when her graciousness was tested, particularly by hostile letters. She wrote, "Nothing so surely takes the wind out of sails like these," and no few were from hostile bishops who had "bones to pick." Often she read only parts of anonymous letters then struck a match and burned them. Then, "I promptly forgot I had ever received it." She explained, "To ignore a wrong is to pour ointment on an abscess."[29]

Her sense of humor. Belle Bennett never laughed *at* a person but laughed *with* them. Her humor charmed her conversations and made strangers feel at ease with her. There was never a trace of sarcasm, although there were numerous opportunities for such.

In 1896, while visiting the Library of Congress—then under construction—one of her party lamented, obviously assuming Belle's attitude, "Think of how many souls could be served in heathen lands by the money invested in this building." Belle retorted, "Think of how many mouths have been fed with money earned in honest toil here."[30]

Her strong conviction of Sabbath observance. Belle Bennett strictly observed the Sabbath. She avoided all travel on Sunday except when at sea. Telegrams or special delivery letters delivered on the Sabbath were not opened until Monday. Sometimes her conviction to this principle required her to stay in a hotel en route to an out-of-town meeting. Mrs. Luke Johnson remembered that Belle "suffered visible pain if long continental or worldwide travel necessitated her continuous going on the Sabbath day."[31]

Simply, there were few things that did not interest Belle Bennett. Besides the major accomplishments already mentioned, she saw the need to stay close to Methodist students on state college campuses and therefore organized Methodist dorms at the universities of Missouri, Texas, and Oklahoma. She organized programs for Cubans in Tampa and Key West. She worked for Prohibition. She was among the first to realize that daily Bible study could be incorporated into the public school curriculum. She called for the Methodists to supply "earnest, well-trained Christian teachers" for the program. She raised funds to build an industrial annex at black Paine College and used the experience to raise the consciousness of Southern women on race.

Still she made time to be "Miss Belle" to hundreds of people. One black preacher said, "Well, bless de Lord, all de ol'time white women ain't dead yet." Josie, her black friend, prayed "morning, evening and noon for Miss Belle."

She never used the pronoun "I" when "we" would do; she never opened a telegram at night, having learned from too many sleepless nights, and she refused to learn to type.

The rich young ruler came to Jesus and turned away at the thought of giving away all his possessions; the rich young Kentucky socialite gave everything to God.

"There must be a great new conception of our stewardship to God if we would have fellowship with Him in service," she wrote. "Money is one of His all-powerful agencies, but without ourselves, our love, our time, it may be made a curse, not a blessing. All things are possible with God, but it is only through man, through the church, that God can do the impossible things for humanity."[32]

Belle Bennett—one of God's remarkable servants—died as she had lived, a servant.

4.

David Brainerd

BORN: April 20, 1718

PROFESSION: Missionary

DIED: October 9, 1747

"He has no more grace than a chair!" On the surface, the
remark sounds inoffensive. Nothing vulgar, obscene, de-
famatory, yet Yale officials were highly incensed by the
words uttered by a young student named David Brainerd.
Those eight words had a profound impact far beyond anyone's imagination. They provoked his immediate expulsion
from Yale and a change of careers which sent him into exile
among the American Indians. Brainerd died young, but in
a few short years he made his way into the church history
books as one of the greatest missionaries of all times.

John Wesley once asked, "What can be done in order to
revive the work of God where it has decayed?" Then he
answered his own question: "Let every Preacher read

carefully the *Life of Brainerd*. Let us be followers of him, as he was of Christ, in absolute self-devotion, in total deadness to the world, and in fervent love to God and man. Let us but secure this point and the world and the devil must fall under our feet."[1]

On April 20, 1718, David Brainerd was born into the Connecticut home of Hezekiah Brainerd, a member of His Majesty's council. From early childhood David was highly emotional, overly self-conscious, and introspective—always terribly concerned for his soul and afraid of dying. He became "very religious" at the age of seven, but he was twenty-one before he felt that he was converted. That fall—1739—he entered Yale in New Haven, Connecticut, to prepare for the ministry.

In his junior year he attended meetings of the New Lights, a group that supported the George Whitefield revival meetings, which were then violently opposed by Yale authorities. In supporting the revivals Brainerd met the spiritual giant Jonathan Edwards, who took an interest in the young student.

That year Brainerd also heard a sermon that would affect the rest of his short life. James Davenport, a thirty-three-year-old single graduate of Yale, criticized, even attacked, New Haven's leading pastor, Joseph Noyes, in the latter's own pulpit. Davenport called Noyes a "sheep in wolves' clothes, an unconverted hypocrite and a devil incarnate."[2] The sermon did wake up the town, but the university quickly reacted to squelch any further criticism of authority. The trustees promptly passed a special resolution "that if any student of this college shall directly or indirectly say that the Rector, either the Trustees or the Tutors are hypocrites, carnal or unconverted men, he shall for the first offense make a public confession in the Hall, and for the second offense be expelled."[3]

Brainerd was one of those students who thought about the consequences of his actions after he had done the deed. University politics were not high on his list of concerns when he attended a Separatist meeting against specific orders of Rector Clap, the school's "president." Another student reported that Brainerd had wondered, aloud, why the rector "did not expect to drop dead" for fining students who had followed Gilbert Tennent, a prominent New England revivalist, to a meeting at Milford. Brainerd denied the last allegation, but it was used against him when another incident occurred.

After prayers one day, a friend asked Brainerd what he thought of Tutor Whittelsey's prayer. Brainerd quipped, "He has no more grace than a chair!" Someone in the hallway (never identified) overheard the remark and reported him to Clap, who called in Brainerd's friends to confirm the story. The taunts appear mild when compared to the protests during the Vietnam War, but nevertheless they were scandalous in the mid-1700s.

Thomas Clap's overbearing nature and his strong opposition to doctrinal innovation, itinerant preachers, lay exhorters, and insolent students motivated him to make an example of Brainerd, whom he expelled.

Entries in Brainerd's diary reflect his mood during the next year or so, as he was privately studying with Jedediah Mills, a strong evangelistic preacher and friend of Jonathan Edwards.

> I seem to be declining with respect to my life and warmth in divine things. . . . Oh, that God would humble me deeply in the dust before Him! I deserve

hell every day for not loving my Lord more, who has, I trust, loved me and given Himself for me.

What are all the storms of this lower world, if Jesus by His Spirit does but come walking on the seas! Some time past, I had much pleasure in the prospect of the heathen being brought home to Christ, and desired that the Lord would employ me in that work. But now, my soul more frequently deserves to die, to be with Christ.

Oh, that I may be always humble and resigned to God, and that He would cause my soul to be more fixed on Himself, that I may be more fitted both for doing and suffering.[4]

Brainerd did not realize how that last phrase would come true. Obviously, the expulsion humiliated him. Fortunately, he thought, his parents were deceased and spared from the embarrassment he would have brought upon them. As he had in his childhood, Brainerd turned inward and isolated himself from the world.

I cried to God to cleanse me from my exceeding filthiness, to give me repentance and pardon. I then began to find it sweet to pray; . . . Found myself willing, if God should so order it, to suffering banishment from my native land, among the heathen that I might do something for their salvation, in distresses and diseases of any kind.[5]

And that was only the beginning of the "weaning" process that turned the quick-tongued student into a saint.

God gave me to wrestle earnestly for others, for the kingdom of God in the world, and for dear Christian friends. I felt weaned from the world and from my own reputation amongst men, willing to be despised and to be a gazing stock for the world to behold.[6]

During this time, Brainerd felt a keen sense of his own faults. He noted that he "appeared exceedingly vile in my own eyes; saw much pride and stubbornness on my part." He despaired that God loved him. "I seemed to feel a sort of horror in my soul," he wrote that spring of 1743. "Alas! When God withdraws, what is there that can afford any comfort to the soul?"[7]

But days of isolation and prayer passed and "the storm" lifted. "I think I scarce ever felt so calm in my life," he scribbled a week after his previous notation. "I rejoiced in resignation and giving myself up to God, to be wholly and entirely devoted to Him, forever."[8]

In reading his diary, one wonders what heinous sins Brainerd could have committed which would have led to such a strong self-denunciation. By the end of the week he had again turned on himself.

Considering my great unfitness for the work of the ministry, my present deadness, and total inability to do anything for the glory of God that way, feeling myself very helpless and at such a great loss for what the Lord would have me do. . . . Oh, I was distressed to think that I should offer such dead, cold services to the living God. My soul seemed to breathe after holiness, a life of constant devotedness to God. But I am almost lost sometimes in the pursuit of this blessedness, and ready to sink, because I continually fall short and miss my desire. Oh, that the Lord would help me hold out, yet a little while, till the happy hour of deliverance comes![9]

Brainerd spent entire days alone, often in the woods praying, fasting, seeking God. Troubled by his fears, he confessed that he was frightened "by the shaking of a leaf." He wrote in his diary, "I could not bear to think of Christians showing me any respect."[10]

Despite his inner turmoil he was preaching on Sundays—in a barn to a few faithful believers—and he preached one Sunday to a small group of Indians near Kent, Connecticut. That day he felt encouraged; he felt God's presence and power, as he spoke from Job 14:14: "If a man die, shall he live again?"

On the day he should have graduated from Yale, Brainerd rode to New Haven to see friends, although he planned to do so privately, not wanting to be seen by the authorities. He had hoped that a group of prestigious ministers would be able to get him reinstated to the university, but Clap had not budged and Brainerd was still an unwelcome visitor.

Brainerd's journal entry that day indicates his mood had again plummeted:

I found some sweetness in the thoughts of bidding a dying farewell to this tiresome world. Though some time ago I reckoned upon seeing my dear friends at commencement, yet being now denied the opportunity for fear of imprisonment, I felt totally resigned and as contented to spend this day alone in the woods, as I could have done if I had been allowed to go into town. Felt exceedingly weaned from the world today.[11]

Was he depressed? Obviously, but only momentarily. By night he wrote,

> I knew not that ever I saw so much of my own nothingness in my life; never wondered so that God allowed me to preach His Word. This has been a sweet and comfortable day to my soul. Blessed be God! Prayed again with my dear friend, with something of the divine presence. I long to be wholly conformed to God and transformed into His image.[12]

The next day, Brainerd snuck into town, preached in the homes of some friends, then escaped back to the farm where he was staying without being "discovered by my enemies."

Thus, when the doors to a traditional ministry closed, Brainerd found that missionaries would not have to pass so close a scrutiny. So he applied for an appointment.

Once he had made his decision to spend his life as a missionary to the Indians, he had no use for the inheritance he had received from his father—a small farm. Brainerd sold the buildings and land and used the money to pay Nehemiah Greenman's way through Yale. Clearly, he held no animosity against the institution and wanted to give someone else the educational opportunity that would never again be in his own grasp. The very next Sunday he preached on Matthew 6:33, "Seek ye first the kingdom of God," surely indicating how earnestly he desired to obey his Lord.[13]

Having burned bridges with the Yale establishment, with his friends, his family, and with the world, Brainerd still struggled with strong negative feelings. On the day he met with representatives of the Society in Scotland for the

Propagation of Christian Knowledge (SSPCK), the missionary organization that would support him, he wrote:

> Alas me thought; how sadly they are deceived in me. How miserably would they be disappointed if they knew my inside! Oh, my heart! And in this depressed condition I was forced to go and preach to a considerable assembly, before some grave and learned ministers; but felt such pressure from a sense of my vileness, ignorance and unfitness to appear in public that I was almost overcome with it. My soul was grieved for the congregation that they should sit there to hear such a dead dog as I preach.[14]

Despite his inner turmoil, Brainerd's preaching was effective. In January 1742, he preached to a badly divided congregation in Stonington. Joseph Fish had pastored that church for ten years, and then, in the summer of 1741, Fish had called a revivalist, Davenport, to hold a meeting. As a result, fanaticism spread like wildfire through the church, and, when Fish opposed the excesses, many of his congregation left.

Under the pressure, Fish became "extremely distressed about his own salvation and conversion" and shared his doubts with his congregation. For six weeks Fish did not preach. But six days after Brainerd preached, Fish returned to the pulpit and his biography assigns partial credit for his recovery to Brainerd, who had preached on humility and obedience to the command that we should love one another.[15]

At the time, New England was torn with debates on revivalism; and Brainerd had the opportunity to talk to pastors and laity on both sides of the issue. The depth of his spiritual sensitivity is portrayed in his disagreement with both factions, noting that "God has not (yet) taught them with briars and thorns to be of a kind disposition towards mankind."

On April 1, 1743, he rode to Kaunaumeek, 20 miles from Stockbridge, New York, where he started his mission work with the Indians. His diary chronicles his first days of ministry.

I was greatly exercised with inward trials and distresses all day. In the evening, my heart was sunk and I seemed to have no God to go to. Oh, that God would help me! (April 1).

Appeared to myself exceedingly ignorant, weak, helpless, unworthy, and altogether unequal to my work. It seemed to me I should never do any service or have any success among the Indians. My soul was weary of life; I longed for death, beyond measure (April 7).

My heart was overwhelmed within me; I verily thought I was the meanest, vilest, most helpless, guilty, ignorant, benighted creature living. And yet I knew what God had done for my soul, at the same time. Sometimes I was assaulted with damping doubts and fears whether it was possible for such a wretch as I to be in a state of grace (April 12).[16]

The Indians received Brainerd cordially and were hospitable. A few were touched by his message. He wrote, "One told me that her heart had cried ever since she heard me preach first."[17]

Brainerd spent his twenty-fifth birthday in the woods, praying and fasting and lamenting the fact "that I have lived so little to the glory of the eternal God." At that particular time he was boarding with a Scottish couple who barely knew English. He was sleeping on straw laid upon boards. Although he was convinced of his call out of "the world," he was desperately lonely.

As an itinerant preacher, Brainerd had no permanent lodging and that contributed to his depression. He welcomed whatever lodging was afforded to him. "I have no fellow Christians with whom I might unbosom myself or lay open my spiritual sorrows; with whom I might take sweet counsel in conversation about heavenly things and join in social prayer."[18]

He was in "foreign" territory on two counts. Both the Indians and the Dutch who had settled the area were suspicious of him.

> My labor is hard and extremely difficult, and I have little appearance of success, to comfort me. The Indians have no land to live on but what these Dutch people lay claim to; and these threaten to drive them off. They have no regard for the souls of the poor Indians; and, by what I can learn, they hate me because I came to preach to them. But that which makes all my difficulties grievous to be borne is that God hides His face from me.[19]

David Wynbeek reported, "Like the Yankee counterpart, the ordinary Dutchman was crassly indifferent to the spiritual needs of his red brother, and along the entire seaboard there was little room and little love for him."[20]

J. M. Sherwood points out that it is difficult for us to understand what Brainerd experienced. He had little or no sense of prayer support.

> Christian missions then had no standing in the American church (and particularly to the Indians). There was little or no faith in them; no prayers were offered for them, either in public or in the closet. There was no public sentiment calling for missions to the heathen and pagan world. Not a dollar was contributed or pledged to the support of missionaries. The few hundreds necessary to support Brainerd came from across the sea.[21]

Slowly, Brainerd began to rely on his interpreter, John Wauwaumpequunaunt, who had been taught to read and write English by another missionary, Stephen Williams. Although he continued to live Indian style, Brainerd moved out of his wigwam into a little hut he had constructed. He established a school and the initial progress of his Indians pleased him.

Brainerd kept rehashing the expulsion from Yale. Wynbeek insists that the Yale incident (in thwarting his desire for scholastic recognition) and the failure of prestigious ministers to get him readmitted overwhelmed him. This may explain why he threw himself into the Indian ministry, in essence, "that I might not be seen or heard of anymore."[22] Brainerd assumed that, in time, Clap would relent and reinstate him, that he would receive his Yale degree. The longer he worked with the Indians, the less he cared about the degree, but the matter still ate at his conscience.

In the fall of 1743, Brainerd wrote a four-hundred-word apology to the trustees, noting in his diary, "God has made me willing to do any thing that I can do, consistent with the truth, for the sake of peace, and that I might not be a stumbling block to others." As a result, Clap agreed to let Brainerd finish his studies but he insisted that he would have to spend his final year in residence at the university. By this time Brainerd did not want to give up his work among the Indians, whom he called "my people."[23]

He found hurdles to the reception of his preaching. One Indian asked him why he was converting Indians to Christianity when the Christians would steal, lie, and drink more than the natives. Yet Brainerd knew that Christ offered them hope. After attending an Indian funeral, he prayed, "Oh that they might be turned from darkness to light," and a burden weighed heavily on his mind at the time of his ordination.[24]

Ebenezer Pemberton preached Brainerd's ordination sermon from Luke 14:23: "And the lord said unto the servant, Go out into the highways and hedges, and compel them to come in, that my house may be filled." Pemberton went on to challenge him:

> What heavenly skill is required, to convey the supernatural mysteries of the gospel into the minds of the uninstructed pagans, who are a people of a strange speech and hard language. . . .
>
> What deep self-denial is necessary to enable you cheerfully to forsake the pleasures of your native country, with the agreeable society of your friends and acquaintances, to dwell among those . . . who inhabit the remotest recesses of the wilderness?

Me thinks I heard you crying out, "Who is sufficient for these things?" You have the divine promise for your security and consolation, "Lo, I am with you always even to the end of the world."[25]

Thus, David Brainerd was ordained, following in the steps of his grandfathers, six great-uncles, a brother and a cousin.

Right after his commissioning he moved west along the forks of the Delaware River. Some Indians had moved farther west in order to escape the white man and more easily hold onto their beliefs in "guiding spirits" in birds and beasts. Other Indians "converted" to the ways of the white man "succumbing to such demoralization that even their religious ideas were confused and incoherent." It seemed Brainerd's work never grew easier.

As the Scots and Germans moved into Indian land as squatters, they forced out the Indians. Brainerd tried but could not procure land for the Indians, who simply were displaced from their tribal lands without compensation. His concern was not only for their spiritual welfare but also for their rights. That concern was not appreciated by many land-hungry colonists.

Naturally there were fears and superstitions that had to be overcome. Some Indians were afraid that, if they embraced the teaching of Brainerd, medicine men would poison them. So Brainerd seized the opportunity to recreate Elijah's test of Baal's prophets:

Confiding in God for safety and deliverance, I bid a challenge to all these powers of darkness, to do their worse upon me. I told my people that I was a Christian and asked them why the powwows [med-

icine men] did not bewitch and poison me. I scarcely
ever felt more sensible of my own unworthiness than
in this action.[26]

Little by little his testimony had effect and Brainerd
looked for God's design in small triumphs. For example,
the day he had forty listeners, he joyously exclaimed, "O
how heart reviving and soul refreshing it is to me to see
the fruits of my labors!" When the Indians asked him to
preach twice a day, he rejoiced that the men were able to
find three deer within close walking distance so that they
could return to hear him preach.[27]

On July 21, 1745, Brainerd baptized his first Indian
converts, Moses Tinda Tattamy (his new interpreter) and
his wife. What a thrilling moment, as he had hired Moses
although he had been a hard drinker and "he seemed to
have little or no impression of religion upon his mind." In
fact, Brainerd lamented, he had seemed "incapable of
understanding and communicating to others many things
of importance."[28]

Was the conversion genuine or merely "convenient"?
Brainerd watched him carefully.

His change is abiding, and his life, so far as I know,
unblemished to this day, although it is now more
than six months since he experienced this change; in
which space of time he has been as much exposed to
strong drink, as possible, in divers places where it
had been moving free as water; and yet has never
that I know of, discovered any hankering desire after
it. . . . I think I have reason to hope that he is
"created anew in Christ Jesus to do good works."[29]

There had been other missionaries among the Indians; what made Brainerd different? One of his early converts explained that Brainerd was the "first white man she could ever love, having suffered so much from them, for she had always been afraid of them."

> She loved David Brainerd very much because he loved his heavenly Father so much that he was willing to endure hardships, traveling over mountains, suffering hunger, and lying on the ground that he might do her people good; and she did every thing she could for his comfort."[30]

As the revival spread, so did the curiosity of white settlers. Brainerd wrote that many came "to hear what this 'babbler' would say to the poor ignorant Indians." Some of the spectators were shaken and converted, but others acted worse than the Indians and distressed Brainerd.[31]

Very early in his ministry Brainerd had to confront the subject of divorce since it was common among the Delawares. One Indian who had left his wife and "taken" another began to struggle with what he should do to make amends. Brainerd insisted that it was the man's duty to renounce his current wife and return to his first, since the first had given him no "just occasion" to leave and had promised to live peaceably with him if he returned. Soon, three or four more couples were reunited, showing Brainerd how genuine revivals do make a difference in a convert's life-style.[32]

This revival could not have been more timely for it broke out just as Brainerd had concluded that he was ineffective as a missionary; he had decided to resign rather than to waste any more of the money of his Scottish supporters.

But instead of leaving in defeat, he organized an indigenous Indian church; he helped the Scottish commissioners perceive the social implications of the Indians' conversion; and he asked them to provide money for resettlement.

Although his ministry was blossoming, Brainerd left "his people" on November 4, 1746. For some time he had been spitting up blood, a recurrence of the tuberculosis he had developed at Yale. When he left the Indians, his brother John took up his work and continued the ministry.[33]

In his illness, Brainerd turned to Jonathan Edwards; under the devoted attention of Edwards's daughter, Jerusha, he quietly corrected his diaries and received visitors. He knew he was dying and that he had been born on a Sunday, even born again on a Sunday. Now he hoped to die on a Sunday. "I long for death," he wrote. "Oh, why is His chariot so long in coming? Why tarry the wheels of the chariot?"[34]

It seemed his relationship with Jerusha was more than patient and nurse. Some scholars suggest that her father edited out some evidence of this in the diaries. Disregarding her father's warnings about the consequences, Jerusha nursed Brainerd through his last days.

On October 4, he spoke to her in a soft voice:

Dear Jerusha, are you willing to part with me? I am quite willing to part with you; I am willing to part with all my friends; I am willing to part with my dear brother, although I love him the best of any creature living. I have committed him and all my friends to God. Though if I thought I should not see you, and be happy with you in another world, I could not bear to part with you. But we shall spend a happy eternity together.[35]

On October 9, 1747, the chariot arrived, and David Brainerd, a mere twenty-nine years old, stepped aboard, although worried that he had dishonored God by his impatience. On Monday, just before the ground froze, he was buried.

What Characterized the Unique Ministry of David Brainerd?

In twenty-nine years what had the Yalie accomplished?
Brainerd did not spend all of his time preaching. He was involved in the founding of Princeton University. He lobbied for the more compassionate recognition of the needs of Indians. His ministry was effective because he lived with them.

Credibility. Brainerd made the great breakthrough in ministry with the Indians because he demonstrated credibility. If Brainerd's policies had been continued, Sherwood lamented, millions of dollars would have been saved and tens of thousands of lives as well, "and the long dark record of injustice, cruelty, perfidy, treaty-breaking, the strong opposing the weak would not have been written."[36]

Devotion to his God. Brainerd was effective—not in masses of Indians converted but in his godly piety. He did not minister to the Indians because there were no other options open to him. He could have had his choice of pulpits across New England; he had good connections with influential leaders. He wanted to be where God wanted him to be.

His diary became a model of devotion to generations of missionaries and ministers (especially Henry Martyn, Phillips Brooks, and Jim Elliot). Few books have had more influence on world missions than his writings, which were published as early as 1746. Jonathan Edwards's *An Account of the Life of the Late Reverend Mr. David Brainerd* became a classic. John Wesley published an abridged version in England in 1768.

Communion with his God. After studying Brainerd's life, J. M. Sherwood concluded that few saints got closer than Brainerd to the throne of God. Brainerd prayed as he rode; in fact, he prayed continuously. He read the Word. Brainerd loved to read and meditate particularly on the prophets of Israel and he chose most of his Old Testament texts from Isaiah and the Psalms. Yet 111 of his 150 sermons were based on ninety-six New Testament texts, sixty-four of which were from the Gospels. As he was dying, someone entered his room holding a Bible. "That dear Book," he gasped, "that lovely Book. I shall soon see it opened. The mysteries that are in it and the mysteries of God's providence will all be unfolded."[37]

Trust in his God. Perhaps it was his expulsion and the subsequent disappointment in himself that shaped his trust in God. Despite his severe and recurring depressions, despite the long days when he felt God had abandoned him, he never really let go of his faith in God. He held on like a boy who cannot swim holds onto a life raft. "I know that I long for God and a conformity to His will, in inward

purity and holiness, ten thousand times more than anything here below."[38]

Sherwood summarized Brainerd's life:

The work done by him in the heart of the American
wilderness and the diary written by him in the
woods, among savages has touched the hearts and
inspired the souls of tens of thousands of God's
children in Scotland, in England, as well as our own
colonies. Here . . . was a life offered up in living
sacrifice for the glory of God and the salvation of
some of the lowest of His creatures.[39]

He also observed:

Little did the solitary, and often lonely and despon-
dent missionary . . . ruminating in his wigwam or log
hut in the forest . . . little did he dream that his life
whose surroundings were so unpromising, whose
scene of labor was so secluded, and whose errors and
shortcomings cost him so many regrets and bitter
tears, would carry light and conviction and stimulus
all over Christendom and down the centuries.[40]

Just as Brainerd did not know the extent of his influence,
so we never quite know what ripples our lives will make.

David Brainerd challenges today's single adult to "seek
first the kingdom of God." One naturally wonders what
would have happened if Brainerd had graduated from
Yale. What if he had not suffered through his own agonies
and been "driven" to serve God?

What a wonderful reminder that God takes our "de-
feats" and uses them as His victories.

5.

Charlotte Digges "Lottie" Moon

BORN: December 12, 1840

PROFESSION: Missionary

DIED: December 24, 1912

A secretary at the Baptist Foreign Mission Board was surprised when a delivery man walked into her office with a small package. "What is it?" she asked, as he placed it on her desk.

"Sign here."

"Well, what is it?" she demanded.

"I don't know. I just deliver the packages." The secretary soon discovered that the small box contained the ashes of Lottie Moon, missionary to China for forty years—a woman the *Foreign Mission Journal* called "the best man among our missionaries."[1]

In the Southern Baptist Convention, Lottie Moon's name is synonymous with missions. Each Christmas they take up an offering for foreign missions; to date, almost one-half billion dollars has been raised in Lottie's honor. Her sacrificial life created the missions awareness that has characterized the Southern Baptists.

Lottie Moon was born December 12, 1840, into a prominent and wealthy Virginia family. Lottie's father, who died when she was 13, became a devout Baptist after a family dispute over the preaching of a Presbyterian turned Baptist, Alexander Campbell. The Moons had overindulged and underdisciplined their children, yet they encouraged strong educational aspirations. Anna Barclay Moon often read stories to her daughter about Ann Judson, the first Baptist woman missionary from America, and tutors came to Viewmont, the family plantation, to teach the children French, the classics, and music. It was just expected that Lottie would grow up, marry well, and spend her life presiding over a large Southern home, full of the sounds of slaves and children.

Lottie's sister Orie was the first daughter to break that pattern; she became the first Southern woman to earn a medical degree. Her "rebellion" opened the door for Lottie to pursue her own goals.

As a child, Lottie was uninterested in religious matters. At the Hollins Institute, she skipped the required chapels 26 times in her last two quarters. At the Albemarle Female Institute in Charlottesville, a progressive female institution, she gained the reputation as both a brain and a heretic. While students admired and followed her, they remained slightly terrified by her.[2]

A bachelor tutor, Crawford Howell Toy, took a strong personal interest in Lottie, his student—not an unusual occurrence at a women's school. Because of his encouragement she took Greek. Perhaps Lottie's spirit and gift for languages fascinated Toy. Whatever, a close relationship developed between them that would last for decades.

Although Lottie paced her class academically, her religious indifference disturbed many students. When one student asked what her middle initial, *D*, stood for, Lottie snapped, "Devil."[3] When John A. Broadus, a prominent Baptist pastor, held a series of evangelistic services for students, Lottie's name ended up on the prayer list.

One morning, Lottie surprised everyone by attending the sunrise prayer meeting; before the series of services was over, she publicly professed her faith in Christ. In those days, the only time a woman could speak in a Baptist church was when she confessed her faith before baptism. So on December 22, 1858, the day after her conversion, Lottie related her story: The night before she attended the prayer meeting, she had been awakened by a barking dog. She had lain awake thinking about her soul and spiritual matters. She resolved to be "open" on the subject. She confessed that she had gone to the revival to scoff.

When Broadus spoke, he always reminded the students and faculty of a commitment to Christian work. Now that she was a believer that theme played differently on Lottie's heart. As one schoolmate noted, Lottie became "God's chosen vessel." She was now submissive to God's voice, ready to do anything He assigned to her.[4]

Broadus's remarks on service, Lottie's own spiritual nature, and a growing awareness in the family that she was old enough to marry created a struggle within Lottie. Already one student had been forced to quit the Albemarle in order to marry someone she did not love. Young ambitious girls often heard the warnings of old maids, "Don't wait too late. This one could be your last chance."

What was God calling Lottie to do? She seriously considered foreign mission work. Up to this point, women had gone to mission fields only as wives, although there was some talk of change in that policy. Even though she didn't know what her future would be, Lottie poured herself into her studies with amazing results. Her Latin examinations were so outstanding that her professor shared them with faculty at the University of Virginia. One professor said that he had "never heard a woman read Greek so fluently and appreciatively." Proficient in Italian, Spanish, and French, Lottie gained the reputation as the most scholarly graduate of Albemarle. Continuing her studies, Lottie Moon became one of the first Southern women to receive the master of arts degree. Broadus enthusiastically labeled her "the most educated woman in the South."[5]

By this time, Virginia was torn by the Civil War. Lottie's dreams and hopes would have to wait for the conflict to end. She returned home to Viewmont, where she was courted by a beau who was waiting for his orders to report as a Confederate chaplain. Although many women were saying yes to men in uniform, Lottie waited. The stories of Ann Judson resonated in her mind. "Ever since that night I went off to scoff at the sermon," Lottie confided in a cousin, "and back to my room to pray, I have wanted to give my life carrying the gospel to the heathen."[6]

The war hit close to Lottie's heart. When rumors claimed that the Yankees were heading for Viewmont, Lottie buried the family silver and jewelry in an orchard. Later, when the fuss blew over and Lottie went back to retrieve the valuables, she couldn't find the spot. So most of the family heirlooms were lost forever. With this loss and the defeat of the South (the Moon money had been converted into Confederate currency), Lottie had to make decisions. Because of the war, the Foreign Mission Board had no money to send anyone out as a missionary. Lottie had to find a job to support herself. She took a teaching job in Danville, Virginia, and also worked as a "pastor's assistant." Later, on the death of her mother, she moved to Cartersville, Georgia, and opened a girls' school.

In 1871, Lottie's eighteen-year-old sister Edmonia, who also had a vision for missions, was appointed a missionary to China. Lottie continued to correspond with the mission board about her own future and she enthusiastically read and reread Edmonia's letters from China. The timing did not seem right for Lottie to go overseas, and she poured herself into the new school and into church work, particularly her Sunday school class, even buying clothes for the girls who could otherwise not attend.[7]

In February 1873, Lottie's pastor, R. B. Headden, preached a stirring missionary message, "Lift up your eyes and look upon the fields for they are white unto harvest," hoping that at least one member might respond. The message touched a chord in Lottie, especially since Edmonia had written, "True, you are doing a noble work at home, but are there not some who could fill your place? I don't know of any who could fill the place offered you here."[8]

At the close of the sermon, Lottie and her close friend A. C. Safford walked down the aisle. Lottie told her pastor, "I have long known that God wanted me to go to China. I am now ready to go."[9] Her determined action created quite a stir in Cartersville.

Lottie had to deal with angry trustees of the school she had just opened. She argued that tuition was too low to make it a going financial concern. They retorted that Lottie would be wasting her life if she went to serve the heathen. Didn't Lottie realize how desperately "good Southern girls" needed an education? Lottie held her ground. At the school's only commencement, the pastor of the Methodist church preached a sermon that confirmed Lottie's decision: "Seek ye first the kingdom of heaven."

On July 7, 1873, Lottie received her appointment and sailed for China.[10]

Upon arrival, she stayed in the home of the Reverend and Mrs. T. P. Crawford, "veteran but eccentric" missionaries. Immediately Lottie expressed her desire to have a home of her own, an idea Reverend Crawford branded as ridiculous. He was convinced that single women should live with married couples, but the Moon sisters quickly perceived that the Chinese viewed such arrangements as polygamous. Lottie wrote home saying, "Stir up the hearts of our sisters in Richmond so they shall build [a house] for my sister and myself."[11]

The Chinese women were curious about Lottie's not having a mother-in-law. "Mothers-in-law are too hard to get along with," Lottie quipped. "I'm afraid she will beat me." The Chinese women laughed, knowing that their lives were controlled by the mothers of their husbands. Even so, no few tried to console Lottie that she had no mother-in-law or husband at "her advanced age."[12]

It did not take long for Lottie to learn to call on the oldest woman in a household; in that way she gained a hearing with all the women. Most hostesses offered her a pipe to smoke, and she always politely refused. In the early days, she was cursed as "foreign devil," but she shrugged off the remark. When she heard the people call her "foreign lady teacher," she knew she was making headway into their hearts.[13]

The major disappointment of Lottie's early years centered around Edmonia's deep depression, which finally incapacitated her. Lottie decided to take her home to Virginia, arriving on December 22, 1876, in time for a great family reunion. Once on her home territory, Edmonia improved and Lottie determined to return to China as soon as possible. Una Lawrence noted, "If the love of the little sister had once influenced her to place her life in China, we can have no doubt that she now turned her face Chinaward because of a conviction in her own heart that there alone she could fulfill God's will for her."[14]

Ignoring every family tie, Lottie wrote the mission board that she was ready to return. But they responded by saying there was no money to send her back. The ladies of the First Baptist Church of Richmond rallied and provided the necessary funds for her return in November 1877.[15] On this trip she traveled as far as Japan with single women sponsored by the Women's Union Missionary Society. Having an interest in their life-style, she stayed with them in Japan and studied the dynamics of their mission compound for single women.

Once in China, Lottie put her Georgian experience to good use and established a girls' school. The woman who had been disturbed about black and white children in Danville, Virginia, and about Sunday school students in Cartersville, Georgia, saw endless opportunities for Chinese children.

Lottie challenged the Chinese prejudice that found little girls' only value in doing menial chores around the home. She reacted bitterly to the custom of footbinding. "Their deformed feet and tottering walk are but a type of their narrow minds and degraded morals. The greatest blessing we could bestow upon this people is the Christian education of the future wives and mothers."[16] Thus, Lottie committed herself to tackling major cultural barriers with long-range solutions rather than immediate and measurable progress.

Lottie had to raise funds for her female students' lodging, food, medicine, and books. But in Lottie's view that was a small price to pay for rescuing some girls from prostitution or virtual slavery. Upper-class families were not, however, easily persuaded. Certainly, there was criticism about Lottie's curriculum. Teaching Christianity, her critics argued, took time away from the classics. And why did girls have to study geography? Lottie wanted to do all she could to expand their worldview. In short, her program worked and paved the way for a reassessment of women's roles in Chinese society.

In her "spare" time, she traveled from neighborhood to neighborhood, teaching in *kangs* (the Chinese combination of living room and bedroom). When people mentioned her "sacrifice" she responded: "Could a Christian woman possibly desire higher honor than to be permitted to go from house to house and tell of a Savior to those who have never heard His name? We could not conceive a life which would more thoroughly satisfy the mind and heart of a true follower of Jesus."[17]

She continued her work with Chinese women, and in remote villages she gathered crowds and then read to them from the Bible and taught them about Jesus.

Time after time, Lottie was a forerunner in her field. Before long, male missionaries were vehemently complaining that she was preaching on those trips. After all, it was their job, not a woman's. The allegation angered her. "If the men do not like the way I am 'sharing the gospel,' let them send some men to do it better." She admitted that she was not ordained but countered she was definitely "foreordained."[18]

Lottie further irritated male missionaries by speaking out on mission policy. They expected the traditional role of silence by women, particularly an unmarried one. Lottie wasn't about to be silenced. She kept up a long, spirited correspondence with the mission board in which she argued her positions. She once declared that "simple justice demands that women should have equal rights with men in mission meetings and in the conduct of their work."[19]

If Lottie would not allow Baptist males to push her around, she certainly would not allow the Chinese. Although she stood only 4-foot-3, she could defend herself, especially with her umbrella, which could be persuasive. In Tengchow, a row of curtains in church separated the women from the men. A new missionary was once asked a question that he could not answer. "I'll ask Miss Moon," he said and proceeded around the curtains. He didn't get far because Lottie herself headed him off with her umbrella. "Mr. Adams! This will not do! The first rule of life in China is that men do not enter where women are."[20]

On another occasion, a soldier riding a horse was intent on running Lottie off the road. She waited until he was almost to her, then she opened her umbrella and waved it before his horse, which bolted and threw the soldier into a small pond. Many people had a healthy appreciation for her umbrella.

The longer she was in China, the more vocal she became in challenging people who offended her. To the adults she replied, "Do not curse me. I am human like you. We are brothers and sisters." When children cursed her she quipped, "To call *me* a devil is to show bad manners." Once she marched an offender off for a frank conversation with his mother. She made it clear to the Chinese that she was there to stay, and that they all had to treat each other with respect.[21]

In time, conflict intensified within the Baptist missionary ranks in China. Crawford, the leader, was traveling through the United States, preaching the concept of self-supporting missions rather than denomination-financed operations. As a result, a split developed in missionary staff, which was exhausted, overworked, and defensive.

But Lottie had her own impact on the view the supporters in the States had of missions. From habit, she had written long letters back home to generate missionary zeal and giving. Her letters, signed "L. Moon," stimulated much interest and enthusiasm among Baptist women. When H. A. Tupper became head of the mission board, he converted that interest into the creation of state women's missionary societies to create a network of support. "Lottie's letter became the curriculum studied by these groups. Each letter was copied and shared many times and was often printed in one of the Baptist state newspapers."[22]

Lottie prodded the Baptists to observe what the Methodists were doing. When she learned that Methodist women had made a commitment to observe the week before Christmas as a time of prayer and giving for missions, she urged Southern Baptists to follow that lead. She wrote a letter explaining why the Christmas season was such an ideal time to set aside money for missions.

Lottie wanted to mobilize the church to give; more money meant more missionaries. She bristled at the suggestion that money be raised by entertainment, bazaars, or gimmicks.

"I wonder how many of us really believe that it is more blessed to give than to receive? A woman who accepts that statement of our Lord Jesus Christ as a fact and not as 'impractical idealism' will make giving a principle of her life. She will lay aside sacredly not less than one-tenth of her income or her earnings as the Lord's money, which she would no more dare to touch for personal use than she would steal. How many there are among our women, alas, who imagine that because 'Jesus paid it all' they need pay nothing!"[23]

Lottie's own commitment to the Word of God may have been the cause of an incredible personal crisis. For years she'd been corresponding with, even been in love with, Crawford Howell Toy, her professor from Albemarle. In the spring of 1879, Toy was forced to resign his post at Southern Baptist Seminary due to allegations of teaching "liberal theories." While no one questioned Toy's character or Christian commitment, his ideas were branded heretical, and Toy ended up teaching at Harvard.[24]

The head of the mission board, knowing of Lottie's romantic attachment, warned her that the board did not agree with Toy's positions on the inspiration of Scripture and that Lottie must not be drawn into the dispute. Lottie's love remained strong and in September 1881, she announced to the China staff that she intended to resign and take the chair of professor of Hebrew at Harvard. Earlier there had been an exchange of letters with Toy about their intent to marry and perhaps serve as missionaries in Japan. Lottie had written her family to prepare for a spring wedding, but that wedding never took place.[25]

Toy remained at Harvard, Lottie in China. Exactly why Lottie did not marry, we do not know. Certainly she was not as liberal as Toy. She had thoroughly studied the controversies and Darwinism and she had seen it as an untenable position. If she felt firmly called to mission work, could she have returned to the Orient with a coworker whose beliefs so differed from her own?

But her biographer Catherine Allen suggests that there may have been other reasons for the broken relationship. Perhaps Toy had overestimated his ability to break Harvard's tradition and gain faculty appointment for a woman. Or maybe she felt tied to China; after all, she was *the* strength of the mission staff in north China. Who could replace her?

Did she ever regret the decision? Apparently not. Years later, Lottie scribbled, "I bless the dear Lord for being with me on this tour now almost ended. He keeps my heart first on Himself and so I have enjoyed the work today."[26]

Across the years, the burden of being a pioneer took its toll on the small woman. Yet no person or event ever seemed to frighten her. When one of her converts was harassed for her Christian witness and called to court, Lottie acted as her attorney. She didn't wait for the proceedings to begin but demanded that the presiding judge read aloud the twenty-ninth article of the treaty between China and the United States; it permitted missionary activity.

When the judge resisted, Lottie accused him of persecuting a widow (a serious violation of Chinese tradition). The accusers, she charged, wanted the widow to pay money to avoid violence.

Lottie stood firm. After all, the treaty gave religious freedom to missionaries and to their converts. She even barged into a sacred temple and announced that if the men of the area did not stop harassing the widow, "all America" would hear about the treaty violation. Later she worried about tarnishing her witness but rationalized that even Paul had asserted his rights as a Roman citizen. She was merely using her American citizenship in a comparable way.[27]

Another incident demonstrates her courage to the Chinese as well as to Baptist leaders. When an antiforeign provincial magistrate orchestrated "trumped up" charges against some Baptists and tortured them, Lottie Moon was outraged—especially when she learned that missionaries would not be protected against future violence, which was increasing at the hands of "Boxers" who roamed the countryside stirring up anti-Christian sentiment.

Ignoring the warnings, Lottie determined to go to the suffering Christians at P'intu. But how could she get to them safely? She hired an enclosed sedan coach and dressed up like a Chinese official—with big rimmed glasses and a man's long robe. She crossed her arms regally in front of her and rode all the way to P'singtu. Although the Christians had been released from jail, she consoled and encouraged them. By risking her life, she won a permanent niche in the hearts of many Chinese.[28]

The Boxers kept up their work, destroying missionary residences, churches, and schools. When the U.S. consul ordered the missionaries onto ships that basically served as refugee camps, Lottie boarded a steamer bound for Japan. For almost a year she taught English in a commercial school, and even there she served as a missionary; since she was allowed to choose her own textbook, she chose the Bible. When things simmered down, she returned to China, the land she loved.[29]

Lottie considered herself "a woman of China" rather than of America. Later in her career she became incensed over the use of the term "heathen," although she had initially used it. She demanded, "Isn't it time that we missionaries part company with those who roll this word *heathen* under their tongues as a sweet morsel of contempt?" Lottie realized that while Anglo-Saxons had been skulking in the forests of Northern Europe, the Chinese had had a viable civilization. "It is time that the followers of Jesus Christ revise their language and learn to speak respectfully of non-Christian peoples." As in many other areas, Lottie wasn't afraid to express her concerns to the mission board members, who eventually saw that she was right.[30]

As engrossed as Lottie was in the Chinese work, she kept an eye on the American support base. Increasingly, the growing indebtedness of the mission board worried her. Why weren't Baptists giving more? The bold mission interest she envisioned would be impossible unless money was available. To see her goal reached, Lottie reduced her own salary and increased her giving. China desperately needed missionaries, she argued, yet the board contended that none could be sent until the debt was paid.

The Chinese economy was also desperate at this time. Around her, Chinese Christians were eating tree bark and sweet potato vines. Again, Lottie denied herself to meet the needs she saw, giving her money to feed the hungry.

In all her years, Lottie had been on furlough only twice. Now, when she was over seventy, the toil affected her mind; she simply stopped eating so that there would be more food for her Chinese students.

As she had once made decisions for Edmonia, her fellow missionaries now decided to send Lottie home for a rest. She was so weak that doctors ordered a special diet to keep her alive until she could reach the States. The cabin steward who carried her aboard the *Manchuria* testified that she weighed only fifty pounds.

A missionary nurse was given a special furlough to accompany Lottie home, but she died in the harbor of Kobe, Japan. Miss Miller, the nurse, notified the captain, and in accordance with Japanese law, Lottie's body was cremated.

Una Lawrence summarized it well: "Lottie Moon, Virginia's gifted daughter, God's precious gift to China, was herself a Christmas gift to heaven on Christmas Eve."[31]

After a lifetime of service in China, the executor sold off her personal property and cleared her bank account of $254. Lottie didn't even have enough money left to pay her way home. She was mourned in China and in Virginia. The Chinese wept, "How she loved us!"

What Characterizd the Unique Ministry of Lottie Moon?

Her conscious awareness of the presence of Christ. Lottie said, "As I wander from village to village, I feel it is no idle fancy that the Master walks beside me and I hear His voice saying gently, 'I am with you always, even unto the end.' "[32]

Catherine Allen, a biographer, observed, "Her most intimate revelations of spiritual life betrayed a near mysticism—constantly experiencing the presence of Jesus Christ. She constantly read the devotional classics and adopted their truths: 'Lord Jesus, Thou are home and friend and fatherland to me.' "[33]

During one tough winter, Lottie alluded to her struggle in her letters home. "I feel my weakness and inability to accomplish anything without the aid of the Holy Spirit. Make special prayer . . . that I may be clothed with power from on high by the indwelling of the Spirit in my heart."[34]

Her sense of call. She cherished her worn copy of Thomas à Kempis's *The Imitation of Christ*. In the margins she had copied other devotional readings in French, German, Latin, Italian, and English. In 1902, after a long, exhausting day, she read from the book: "There is nothing else that I am able to present more acceptable than to offer my heart wholly to God, and to unite it most inwardly unto Him."[35]

She underlined the last sentence and wrote the date and the name of the village in the margin. Again, a reminder of that walk down an aisle in a Baptist church so many years before.

Remember that China was a difficult mission area. Several times the missionaries had to retreat for their own personal safety. Many Westerners were emotionally destroyed by their work. One Presbyterian leader said, "No man, lay or cleric, will hold out in this place without a clear call of God to labor for the souls of men."[36] Yet Lottie held on—despite that fact that many Baptists believed that God would never call a woman to be anything other than a wife and mother. What could a woman expect? they'd ask. Weren't Lottie's problems consequences of her own choices? Maybe they were, but she felt they were God's choices for her.

Her deep commitment to the Word of God. Lottie Moon's competency in reading Greek and Hebrew did not help her learn Chinese, but that knowledge was helpful in stimulating her mind. For example, two single women, Ella Jeter and Ida Taylor, lived with the 60-year-old Lottie for several months in 1905. Each day they had devotions together. One particular day, as Lottie read aloud, the girls looked at each other. Perhaps she was getting senile. What she was saying did not correspond with their Bibles. When one of them finally asked, "What are you reading from?" Lottie quipped, "The Greek," and kept right on reading.[37]

She deeply loved the Word of God and prodded her students to memorize large portions of it. In the margin of her Bible she wrote, "Words do not fail to express my love for this holy Book, my gratitude for its Author, for His love and goodness: how shall I thank Him for it!"[38]

Only eternity will tell us whether or not her concern for God's Word was the issue that kept her from marrying Toy. It seems her decision was based on a conflict of interests.

When a young relative once asked Lottie if she had ever been in love, Lottie answered, "Yes, but God had first claim on my life and since the two conflicted there could be no question about the result."[39]

Her love for children. Lottie Moon had a deep love for children. She missed her interaction with her nieces, nephews, and those she might have had by marriage. Lottie frequently corresponded with American children in missionary groups called Sunbeams, and she responded when children wrote to her. Children so identified with her that two even sent her part of their Christmas money. She admitted, "One misses a good deal in losing the childhood of the young people among one's relatives, and

I am especially fond of children. But, among the Chinese, I have the reputation of being a lover of children."[40]

Lottie never forgot her Virginia recipes; she often baked and was known for her cookies. At first, Chinese children (and their mothers) were alarmed, fearing the cookies contained poison. But eventually the delicious aroma overpowered their fears. When she appealed for missionaries she always asked for more single women, specifying that they not be young and that they like children.[41]

Her humor and her lively spirit. Lottie had an incredible gift of laughter, especially in regard to customs. She saw the comical in incidents others may have seen as disastrous. For example, before she knew the language very well, she was telling the story of David to some children. She explained that David had killed the lion, but she incorrectly inflected on the word for *lion*.

"Oh, that is nothing," one boy piped. "I kill them every day—more than one!" Lottie was speechless, but then realized that she had used the word for *vermin* rather than *lion*. No wonder her Chinese students thought nothing extraordinary in the account of David's bravery.[42]

Even dying, she expressed her liveliness. As they got her ready to carry to the coast, the doctor said, "Just lay down, dear Miss Moon." She didn't and he repeated his command. "Lay down, *now*." Suddenly the old Lottie quipped, "I will not lay down, sir, but I will *lie* down."[43]

Her loneliness. At the end of her life, Lottie Moon wrote, "I pray that no missionary will ever be as lonely as I have been." To have had such a brilliant mind and no one with whom to talk or banter had created an awesome loneliness. How did she respond? She persistently pled that the mission board send more women to China, but she also accepted that loneliness.

"I console myself by thinking that one can't have all the good things and that those I long for are in God's loving care. My life is too full for such longings."[44]

After Viewmont was sold and Edmonia died, there was nothing to entice her back to Virginia. Even in her old age, when people urged her to retire, she only responded, "Nothing could make me stay. China is my joy and my delight. It is my home now."[45]

Her hospitality. Lottie's Southern hospitality always shone through her work. Her home became a welcome refuge for weary, sick, or lonely missionaries, and she never turned away a beggar. Since she considered hospitality a Christian grace, hundreds of Chinese enjoyed her openness in the course of a year.

There is no doubt Lottie shaped the course of Southern Baptist missions, even though she was half a world away from her Virginia home. Single women missionaries are especially indebted to her for proving—by word and by deed—that women could carry their weight in the work of the Lord.

Lottie Moon, a single adult, changed the shape of missions.

6.

Correman "Corrie" ten Boom

BORN: April 15, 1892, Amsterdam

PROFESSION: Evangelist/writer

DIED: April 15, 1983

After the audience's response to the music, Corrie knew it was going to be a tough assignment. The shrieking, yelling, and screaming intensified. "Lord, must I speak in this place? I cannot," she said firmly.

The noise grew worse as she began to speak; the prisoners tossed benches.

Corrie shouted above the din, "When I was alone in a cell for four months. . . ."

Suddenly, there was silence. This little old grandmotherly woman, a prisoner? Impossible. The inmates pushed forward for a closer look at this Dutch woman who had come to speak to them. The message, like most of Corrie's, had a theme: "There is no pit so deep that Jesus is not deeper still."[1]

Her roots were thoroughly Dutch. Born in 1893, her father was a watchmaker in Amsterdam. In 1918, Corrie became the first licensed woman watchmaker in Holland and joined her father in a shop that had been owned by ten Booms for a century. Corrie said, "My desire to please my papa was one of the basic motivations of my life." Papa had exacting standards, regardless of the customer's social status or wealth. He reminded his daughter that God was concerned about her work as a watchmaker.[2]

That was illustrated when she learned the extent to which her father would go with his values. Casper ten Boom was not a money-maker. Once when a large bill had to be paid, a wealthy customer walked into their shop and picked out an expensive timepiece. "This is just what I have been looking for." Corrie realized that with such a sale the bill could be paid, and perhaps a little left over.

In talking with Mr. ten Boom, the man explained that he had been displeased with the work of another watchmaker named van Houten from whom he had bought a defective watch.

"Let me see the watch." Caspter ten Boom made some adjustments on the watch and gave it back to the customer. "It will be fine." Then he added, "Sir, I trust the young watchmaker . . . you can encourage him by buying the new watch from him."

Corrie (and the customer) couldn't believe their ears. "Papa! How could you?" Her father reminded Corrie that he had preached the young watchmaker's father's funeral, as he did for all the watchmakers in Haarlem.

"Corrie, what do you think that young man would have said when he had heard that one of his good customers had gone to Mr. ten Boom? Do you think that the name of the Lord would be honored? There is blessed money and cursed money. Trust the Lord. He owns the cattle on a thousand hills and He will take care of us."

Corrie knew it would do no good to continue her "Yes, buts."[3]

Corrie learned about her father's stern side when she first refused to go to school. Angrily, Corrie tightened her fingers in a white-knuckled grip on the stair railings. Casper ten Boom bent over her, and one by one, loosened Corrie's fingers. Corrie howled her protests, but her father all but dragged her to school. He kissed her and assured her that when school was over, he would be waiting for her.[4]

Although she enjoyed her job in the watch shop, she believed there was more to be done. "Dear Lord," she often prayed, "can You use me in some way?" As her aunt quipped, "Corrie always tried to do five or six jobs." She started several clubs for young girls, including a Christian scouting movement called The Triangle Girls, designed to meet the gap between Sunday school (in Holland, for young children) and the YWCA for young women. As soon as the shop was closed, Corrie would eat a quick dinner, then rush off to the club meetings.[5]

Later Corrie organized *Vriendenkring* or Club of Friends, for both young women and young men, so controversial that the experiment was kept quiet for a full year. Many marriages resulted from the group.

Corrie was also involved in starting programs for the mentally handicapped. Many could not attend church; few could understand a sermon. Because they needed to know Jesus, Corrie took on the responsibilities of organizing "a special church" on Sunday afternoons for them.

She helped prepare young women for church membership. The Dutch took their catechism seriously but the old-fashioned, complicated style of language confused many.

Corrie found a way to explain it. She was so successful that one minister declared, "I'll never examine Corrie ten Boom's confirmands and mine together again. I've seldom been so ashamed of the poor results of my teaching."[6]

The ten Boom family took in foster children. Their love of children was noted by one missionary, who had to deal with a child that could not be easily placed. "Send her to the Beje (the ten Boom home), they always have more room. If they don't, they will make it."[7]

However, the life of the ten Booms changed dramatically when the Germans invaded the Netherlands in 1940. Corrie and her family listened in horror as the Queen gave her farewell words to the Dutch people. This was the moment that could not happen. The Dutch had watched the geography of Europe change with Hitler's rise to power, but few had assumed he would invade Holland. The German occupation became another "opportunity" for witnessing. When the occupation forces stepped up their anti-Jewish discrimination, the ten Booms intensified their long tradition of love and service for the Jewish people.

That led to their involvement with underground resistance. Pam Rosewell, one of Corrie's companions, wrote that the ten Booms were not afraid of facing the consequences of their convictions and actions.[8] Throughout the resistance, word got out that the Beje was a "safe" place. Corrie directly supervised the hidings. Eventually, the ten

Boom home became known as the happiest underground address in the Netherlands.

So many people under one roof and the fear of discovery created problems.

Emergencies added to the tension; when a Jewish woman was about to give birth, a doctor and a hospital had to be found (a difficult task). And acts of kindness toward Jews were punishable. Soon, a secret room was built, adjacent to Corrie's bedroom, to hold eight people.

Every night the guests-in-transit had to take all their clothing and possessions into the Anglecrib (as the hiding place was called). Corrie organized drills to see how quickly the "guests" could make it to the secret room, which might be necessary at any hour of the day or night. The Nazis' favorite times to raid were mealtimes and in the middle of the night. Corrie had to expect a raid at any time.

The first rehearsal was pandemonium as eleven people raced for shelter. Corrie hastily rearranged the chairs at the dining room table to look as though only three had been eating. The drill took four minutes. Too long.

Then the underground contact produced what the Nazis would have found incriminating evidence: two spoons and a piece of carrot on the steps, pipe ashes in an "unoccupied" bedroom. That would arouse the curiosity that could lead to imprisonment and death.

The next drill was cut to two minutes, twenty-seven seconds; by the fifth drill, the time was two minutes, flat. Meanwhile, Corrie worked to learn "stalling tactics" that might give the guests another seventy seconds.[9]

There were other pressures also, such as with the rationing of food and feeding so many guests, or a guest who was asthmatic. Corrie fretted when she could still hear the wheezing through the wall. Other hosts had refused this seventy-seven-year-old woman, Corrie could not. Worse, the woman had difficulty climbing the stairs. That could risk the lives of the others. Corrie put the issue to a vote. The "family" of nine voted that the woman stay.[10]

Day after day, month after month, Corrie sold watches and worked for the resistance, all the time waiting for the Gestapo. The stressful tranquility of the Beje changed on February 28, 1944. A man knocked on the door pleading to talk to Corrie. He explained that his wife had been arrested for helping the Jews. Surely she would be killed. Would Corrie help? How? There was a policeman who could be bribed, who would set her free for six hundred guilders.

The word went out through Corrie's network that she had to have the money within an hour. Corrie, weak with fever, returned to bed, confident that the money would come, and it did.

Five minutes after Corrie gave him the money, the Gestapo raided. Four Jewish refugees and two underground workers dashed through Corrie's bedroom into the secret place. Corrie threw a briefcase of records into the room and fell back into bed, just as a German soldier barged in demanding, "Where is your secret room?"

This was no drill. The Gestapo knew there were Jews in the house. "Never mind," he snapped. "We'll have the house watched until they're turned into mummies." There had not been time to turn the "all-safe" sign in the window; more people stumbled into the Gestapo trap. A total of thirty-five people were arrested. (The Jews remained hidden for three days but were eventually led to safety.)

After interrogation at Gestapo headquarters, the ten Booms were taken to Scheveningen prison. Corrie kissed her father, "The Lord be with you." Casper whispered, "and with you, my daughter." He died ten days later.

Corrie was soon isolated from other prisoners, for fear that she might be developing TB. She was alone for the first time in her life; she befriended ants in her cell to keep her sanity.

Corrie dared ask her judge, Hans Rahms, "Is there any darkness in your life?" Five times she prayed with him. Her influence led him to free her brother William and then destroy papers that would have incriminated many underground workers and Jews.[11]

On June 6, Corrie found her sister Betsie among a group of prisoners being transferred to the dreaded Ravensbruck, where nearly 96,000 women died. On Christmas 1944, Betsie died. Through a clerical error, Corrie was released and returned home, a broken fifty-two-year-old woman.[12]

Concentration camp had not changed Corrie's thinking. On her way home Corrie expressed her gratitude for life. "Lord, I have received my life back from You. Thank You. Will You tell me how to use it? Give me understanding. . . . My work must be to save souls for eternity to tell about You."[13]

When the war ended, Corrie worked to organize a center at Bloemendaal, to help European refugees. Although there was plenty to do, Corrie experienced a growing conviction that she was to go to America.

In Ravensbruck, she and Betsie had talked about their future. "God showed me," her sister said, "that after the war we must give to the Germans that which they now try to take away from us: our love for Jesus." Corrie was stunned.

"Oh, Betsie," Corrie groaned, "you mean if we live we will have to return to Germany?"

115

"Corrie," Betsie said calmly, "there is so much bitterness. We must tell them that the Holy Spirit will fill their hearts with God's love."[14]

Betsie then revealed that she had prayed that after the war God would give them one of the concentration camps to use for ministry. Corrie hesitated. *If I ever get out of here, I will go home to repair and sell watches. I never want to step foot in Germany again. Never!*

Betsie challenged Corrie's resentment. "The Germans are the most wounded of all the people in the world." Corrie's mind reeled with the possibilities. "Only God could see in such circumstances the potential for ministry in the future—ministry to those who even now were preparing to kill us."

Betsie added, "We will travel the whole world bringing the Gospel to all—our friends as well as our enemies."

"To *all* the world? But that will take money," Corrie, always the practical one, confronted her.

"Yes, but God will provide. We must do nothing else but bring the Gospel and He will take care of us. After all, He owns the cattle on a thousand hills. If we need money we will just ask the Father to sell a few cows."[15]

The "whole world" included America.

One year after her release from prison, Corrie ten Boom sailed to America with fifty dollars in her purse. Many had questioned her decision. "It's not easy to make one's way in America."

"Yes," Corrie agreed, "but God has directed me and I must obey." Not everyone greeted Corrie with open arms. Some suggested she should have stayed in Holland. During those years, Corrie grew to rely on the provision of God for all her needs.

Over the next twenty years, Corrie became involved with Brother Andrew's work in smuggling Bibles behind the Iron Curtain. She said, "There is no limit to what He will do for us and no end to his blessings, if we surrender to Him. Surrender is trusting God."[16] Slowly Betsie's vision came true: Corrie became "a Tramp for the Lord." The entire world was her parish. In declining one request to speak, she wrote, "In January and February I expect to be in Formosa, in March and April in Australia and New Zealand, part of April and May in South Africa, and in Palestine and Spain in June. All this, of course, God willing."[17] Often she had only enough money to get to one place, but she trusted the Lord to provide money to get to the next place.

In 1968, she became involved with Billy Graham, who called her "God's merry saint." By now, thousands were reading her books, starting with *A Prisoner and Yet*, published in 1954. Two American writers read her memoirs and were convinced she had a story to tell. John and Elizabeth Sherrill helped her write *The Hiding Place*, which sold over 2 million copies.[18]

Naturally people asked, "and after that what?" so Corrie next wrote about her years as a *Tramp for the Lord*.

Ruth Graham saw the movie possibilities in *The Hiding Place*. Movies had not been part of Corrie's tradition, but she came to understand that this medium would vastly extend her ministry and fulfill Betsie's vision. The filming experience was demanding for it forced her to confront many painful memories. When it was premiered in Hollywood in September 1975, her physician, David Messenger had to escort her from the screening. It was too overwhelming.[19]

Over 15 million saw the film and Corrie, by then in her eighties, found herself "the darling of American evangelicals and the most sought after woman speaker in the world."[20]

At age eighty-four, Corrie ten Boom felt the Lord she had so long followed as his tramp was leading her into a new ministry, again, in America. She told Pam Rosewell, "I am nearly eighty-four now and I am at a crossroads in my life. I have asked the Lord to give me a new ministry and I believe He will do it. I do not know what it is yet, but He will show me."[21]

In April 1978, fearful of a Russian invasion in Europe, Corrie moved to California. At her age, travel was a burden. She wrote,

> I always had the grace to be a tramp, and whenever I felt sorry for myself I would say, "Lord Jesus, You suffered so much for me. If I have to suffer just a little bit for You, I will." And I was happy in the work the Lord had given me. But now that I am no longer a tramp, I am so happy to have my own home and believe it will be very fruitful in the Lord's service. Pray for the books that will be born here.[22]

The Lord had told Corrie that she would write five books and do five movies. That's quite an agenda for an eighty-five-year-old but no one dared dispute her "the Lord has told me."[23]

She worked hard in what many thought was retirement. "The Lord has first place in this house. He has given us much important work to do here, and it is because we are doing His will that He blesses the home. Apart from the writing of books and the making of films, there is intercession from this house, plus counseling personally and by telephone and letter."[24]

In 1977, she had heart surgery and a pacemaker was installed, after she decided it was all right for a child of God to want to live longer. She had been taunted by a dream of another prison; a prison she could not escape. She understood that dream whan a stroke in 1978 limited her ability to speak and to travel.

For five years she endured what Pamela Rosewell called "the silent years." Then on April 15, 1983, she slipped peacefully into the presence of Christ. Everyone's grandmother, God's merry saint, had been one single adult who made a difference.

What Characterized the Unique Ministry of Corrie ten Boom?

Corrie ten Boom was an incredible woman: writer, speaker, filmmaker, friend. In talking to her friends and associates, it is amazing to hear what people consider to be the key to her life.

Her deep personal faith. Corrie's faith was shaped by her parents. Corrie learned theology through her father's eyes. Casper ten Boom believed in the grace of God and that we are all sinners saved by Grace. However, another strong influence on young Corrie was her Aunt Jans, a never-married who lived in the house and who insisted that we are saved by works. Corrie sided with her father. Although the ten Booms attended the cathedral near their home, Casper was dismissed by many as too conservative.

Casper early introduced his children to the Bible and encouraged them to memorize Scripture in different languages.

Corrie had a strong commitment to Scripture. Once, while talking to some prisoners, she seemed stumped as to how to get through to them about her faith. So she took a box of chocolates and shared them. What a luxury! Then she said, "No one has said anything to me about the chocolate."

"Oh, yes, we thanked you."

"But no one questioned me about this chocolate. No one asked whether it had been manufactured in Holland, or what quantities it contained of cocoa, sugar, milk, or vitamins. You have done exactly what I intended you to do: You have eaten and have enjoyed it." Corrie quickly moved to drive home her point.

"It is just the same with this book. If I read the Bible in a scientifically theological or scholarly way it does not make me happy. But if I read in it that God so loved the world that He gave His only begotten Son . . . then I am happy."[25] Corrie called memorizing verses her "First Aid Course," emergency Scriptures "which I apply to a [spiritual] wound until I can look up the rest of the Scriptures which will bring further healing."[26]

Corrie taught that the Bible could be trusted. "If we diligently read the Bible, the Holy Spirit will give us the right words and Scripture references,"[27] a principal she had adopted from her father who quoted Isaiah 50:4 as a basis for the practice. "The Lord God hath given me the tongue of the learned, that I should know how to speak a word in season to him that is weary. . . ."[28]

Corrie had five reasons why she believed the Bible is inspired:

1. It says so.

2. The effect it has on people who follow it.

3. The agreement of the writers, despite their difference in time frames.

4. The authors did not offer any excuses for their own faults or sins.

5. The writers recorded some of the most harrowing scenes, which affected them greatly, yet they never expressed one word of emotion. The Holy Spirit wanted the facts recorded, and not their feelings about the facts.

Simply, the Word of God was an unshakable foundation for the Christian.[29] Corrie could hide Jews in her attic and risk her life because she believed that Scripture taught that Jews were God's chosen people. Even though other Christians disagreed or refused to become involved in the effort, the point was not negotiable to Corrie.

Her commitment to prayer. Corrie's exposure to prayer came early, from her father who daily prayed for the queen and the Second Coming. Corrie said that her father prayed "because He had a good Friend to talk over the problems of the day." Simply, "he talked to someone he knew."[30]

At her memorial service, her good friend, Cliff Barrows, observed,

No one ever had a private conversation with Corrie. I've talked to her alone, but I always had the sneaking suspicion that there was someone else listening in on her side—that was her blessed Lord. The unseen guest at every meal and the silent listener to every conversation was a day-by-day fact and reality to Corrie. More often than not she would all of a sudden say, "Now, Father, You have heard what we have been talking about. You know the need. We thank You for listening. We thank You for caring. And we trust You to supply us. Hallelujah. Amen."[31]

Billy Graham's niece recalled one such experience. Debbie Ford said, "I seemed to hear the Lord say, 'And Corrie, what can I do for you today?' She was constantly expected."[32]

Corrie often said, "Never doubt that God hears our prayers, even the unusual ones." Yet, many people are too impatient; they conclude that God has said *no*. Many times the answer was: *wait.*[33]

Behind Corrie's attitude on prayer was simple belief: "We never know how God will answer our prayers, but we can expect that He will get us involved in His plan for the answer. If we are true intercessors, we must be ready to take part in God's work on behalf of the people for whom we pray."[34]

Pam Rosewell, Corrie's companion for five years, wrote of those concluding moments at the end of a day when she prayed. Corrie always included this idea: "Father, will You keep us so close to Your heart that even our dreams are peaceful, and that we see things as it were more and more from Your point of view."[35]

Her love of children. Corrie admitted that even though she and Betsie never married, the Lord certainly blessed them with children. Her first exposure to other people's children was when the ten Booms cared for a group of German children sent to Holland to recover from the effects of World War I.

As a child, Corrie had shared an idea of keeping the children of missionaries who, for whatever reason, could not live with their parents in the mission field. The idea pleased Corrie's mother.

Years passed before a missions organization asked the ten Booms to keep some children of missionaries until other arrangements could be made. Eventually eleven such children lived in the Beje, sometimes as many as seven at a time. Years later, one of them said, "I still thank God that He gave me these substitute parents . . . and that I was privileged to live with the ten Booms during those important years."[36]

Hans lived with Corrie for a number of years and said, "She gave to many girls what is most precious for this life, for they might never have heard the Gospel if it had not been for her." Simply, there were hundreds of young people, through their clubs, who found direction for their lives through Corrie's influence.[37]

Her love of people. There were few strangers to Corrie. Many people immediately thought of her as a grand-mother. When she was a child, her Father had prayed for the queen. In 1956, while in Formosa, Dr. Bob Pierce of World Vision told her she should talk to the queen.

Corrie dismissed the idea as the idle talk of an American who knew nothing about protocol. A commoner ring the queen's doorbell? Unthinkable. Yet, when she got home she did write the queen a letter. The next day found a limousine waiting to carry her to the palace. After meeting the queen and several other people in the palace, Corrie excused herself, explaining that she was leaving for Germany.

"Oh, but I was expecting you to stay several weeks here. Why are you going to Germany?" (Although the war had been over a long time, there was still a great deal of bitterness toward the Germans.)

Without blinking an eye, Corrie answered: "I must go to Germany, your highness. Because God has called me to tell them of His love and forgiveness." She later returned and each day spent an hour talking with the queen. Corrie wrote, "I believe that in some way something of Father's prayers was answered when God allowed the daughter of a watchmaker to carry His message of love to the Queen."[38]

Corrie also liked commonfolk. My friend David Messenger tells about the time when Corrie stayed at his house and the hot water heater leaked. Corrie followed the firemen who came to clean up the water, asking, "Do you know Jesus? He is my friend."[39]

Her sense of self-esteem. Billy Graham not only called her one of God's "merry saints," he also called her one of God's greatest saints, yet she had friends who kept her feet on the ground.[40]

A prophet is without honor in his own country and Corrie certainly experienced that. She said of Holland, "It is difficult to preach here." Simply, the Dutch were not as open to her messages of forgiveness nor as appreciative of the tramping she did. When Corrie found herself a "star" with the movie, best-selling books, and thousands hearing her speak, she became concerned. Corrie wrote, "The friendly and even sincere words, 'I enjoyed your message' are not the only result I want to attain."[41]

An experience in Cuba impacted her. The church was filled with the most prominent people in Havana; the parish magazine had a glowing article about her. "Corrie ten Boom is a most popular world evangelist. . . . She is tireless and completely selfless in her absolute dedication to the cause of the Gospel."

Corrie struggled. *Oh, Lord, if only these people knew who the real Corrie ten Boom is, they would not have come out this morning to hear me.*

To which the Lord replied, "Tell them."

"But Lord, if I tell them, they will reject me."

"Can I bless a lie?"

Corrie took her introduction that day from the parish paper. Looking at the congregation, she said, "Sometimes I get a headache from the heat of the halo that people put around my head."[42]

That experience *before* her fame shaped her response to the fame.

Sometimes, her Dutch could be quickly stirred. Amateur photographers could annoy her. To one she said, "I'm talking about the Lord, not me."[43]

Corrie did not place much stock in possessions, perhaps from living so long out of a suitcase. Remember the incident of her father's prying her fingers from the stairs. Later in prison, when she stripped naked, she clung to her Bible. Possessions meant nothing in Ravensbruck. Corrie later said, "I have learned in my years on earth to hold everything loosely, because when I hold them tightly, God has to pry my fingers away, and that hurts."[44] If it didn't have eternal life, Corrie didn't worry about it. When Pam broke a prized china vase, Corrie remarked, "Child, don't worry about it. It hasn't got eternal life."[45]

Corrie had received so many compliments: "Oh, you were so brave!" Or "what a great talk!" Other spiritual leaders would have begun believing their press releases, but not Corrie. She explained, "I take each remark as if it were a flower. At the end of the day I lift up the bouquet of flowers I have gathered throughout the day and say, 'Here Lord, it's all Yours.' "[46]

Her singleness. The love that Corrie had for a man named Karel is well known by those who have read her books.

In earlier years, people asked, "Were you ever in love?" When her girls in the Triangle Club asked her, Corrie would lightly scold, "You rascals, asking me that!"

Corrie loved Karel and assumed they would marry; his mother decided otherwise. She wanted him to marry a rich woman who could help his career in the church. Corrie had little warning that Karel's feelings for her had changed until one day when he appeared on the Beje doorstep, with a young woman. He said, "Corrie I want you to meet my fiancée." Corrie's world trembled, yet in polite Dutch fashion she was hospitable. "Somehow I managed to shake her hand, then Karel's hand, and to wish them every happiness. . . . Before the door shut I was fleeing up the stairs. . . ."

She cried for a long time. Eventually, her father came up, as he had so many times to tuck her in. "But this was a hurt that no blanket could shut out, and suddenly I was afraid of what Father would say. Afraid he would say, 'There'll be someone else soon,' and that forever afterward this untruth would lie between us. For in some deep part of me I knew already that there would not—soon or ever—be anyone else." A wise father tenderly reminded

Corrie that love was the strongest force in the world. "When it's blocked that means pain. There are two things we can do when this happens. We can kill the love so that it stops hurting. But then of course part of us dies too. Or, Corrie, we can ask God to open up another route for that love to travel."

By her own admission she was "still in kindergarten in these matters of love." But Corrie recognized her task: to give up her love for Karel. She prayed, "Lord, I give to You the way I feel about Karel, my thoughts about our future—oh, You know! Everything! Give me Your way of seeing Karel instead. Help me to love him that way. That much."[47]

Corrie often shared that experience with the young women in her clubs. Her lifelong prayer became, "I want, Lord, to belong to You with my body, soul, and mind. I claim Your victory, Lord Jesus, over that wound which is hurting me. Let Your victory be demonstrated also in my sex life."[48]

Years later, Corrie told her physician, "I told the Lord He would have to help me. That He had made me a woman . . . with feelings. And He did."[49]

All of these elements blended to make Corrie an effective servant.

What Were Corrie's Accomplishments?

Corrie was an incredible war-horse. Her schedule dizzied many of her closest friends. She explained, "Many times I did not know why I was to go to a certain place until I arrived. It had become almost second nature not to make my plans and then ask for God's signature. Rather,

I learned to wait for God's plan and then write my name on the schedule."[50]

Once, in Israel, a flight attendant condescendingly patted her hand. "Now, lady, don't be afraid. I've flown in thirty-four countries in the last ten years, and nothing ever happened."

It was a challenge Corrie could not pass up. "Sir," she said, "I have ministered in over sixty-four countries, and nothing ever happened . . . so don't *you* be afraid."[51]

Corrie modeled servanthood. Pam Rosewell learned about servanthood one day when she strongly protested Corrie's scheduling, specifically, that she had agreed, on the eve of leaving for a major trip, to meet with a young man.

Firmly, patiently, Corrie stared at Pam. Many times, her look and silence was more effective. "God has sent this young man, and we will receive him. Child, you have to learn to see things in the right proportions. Learn to see great things great and small things small."[52]

That sums up her ministry: Corrie ten Boom was able to spot the great things and to ignore the small things. For example, she turned down the invitaton of the Rose Bowl Committee to be Grand Marshal of the Rose Parade. The Rose Parade! Carlson noted, "With a mere shrug of her shoulder and her frequent expression, 'I don't think that's important.' " Not a hard decision for a woman who "wore the world like a loose garment that she could step out of at will."[53]

Corrie lived by this axiom: "All that we do through our own strength has to be cleansed, but what we do through the Lord has value for time and eternity."[54]

Corrie reminded the church of the commitment of taking the Gospel to all people. Corrie once said, "It is such a joy to know that the Holy Spirit doesn't need a high IQ in a person in order to reveal Himself." God gave Corrie ten Boom a great love for exceptional children. In fact, in *In My Father's House* she prodded her readers, "Whenever you come into contact with feebleminded people, please tell them that Jesus loves them. They often understand God's love better than people who have problems because of their intellectual doubts."

Corrie ten Boom, friend of Billy Graham, house guest of the queen of the Netherlands, was equally at home with handicapped children like Henk, a child from whom Corrie learned much about the workings of the Holy Spirit.

Corrie visited in Henk's home. After talking with his mother, Corrie went upstairs and found Henk kneeling in front of a picture of Jesus on the cross. He was singing: "Out of my bondage, sorrow and night, Jesus I come, Jesus . . . I come to Thee."

Corrie reflected on that moment, "I've heard Bach played by Schweitzer and anthems sung by gigantic choirs, but at that moment I felt as if I were in a cathedral with angels surrounding me. I tiptoed back downstairs without disturbing him, praising God for the love He brings into the lives of 'even the least of them.' "[55]

Pam Rosewell wrote that work with the handicapped prepared Corrie for her own final "silent years." Americans' self-image, Pam noted, is tied intricately to their work and productivity. "But what happens when a person becomes old, frail, brain-damaged, and in some eyes, apparently useless?"

Pam saw this after Corrie's second stroke. How could this great speaker and writer serve God or be of use to

Him now? "A new awe for the preciousness of human life came into our thinking. God had made mankind in His own image. He had made Corrie ten Boom in His own image. *Whether young, old, strong, weak, well, ill, she was equally precious in His sight. His view of her had not changed although in the eyes of an achievement oriented society she may have lost her usefulness.*"[56]

Even in her silence she taught.

Corrie reminded the world of the needs of the Jews. The world has a short memory. There is a generation of Americans too young to remember World War II and the Holocaust. Corrie's heroic action in hiding Jews says a great deal about the role of the Christian in an unjust society. Corrie prodded the evangelical consciousness. There was a time for Bible studies and prayer meetings but there was also a time for risk taking.

Her heroism earned her a place on the Israeli government's list of "righteous gentiles." When others were denied the opportunity to minister in Israel, Corrie ten Boom was welcomed.

By reminding us that it had once happened, she warned us that it could happen again. She was not a daredevil, but a Christian who stood in the gap.

Corrie demonstrated a practical model for sharing and witnessing. Corrie ten Boom was a storyteller. She looked for object lessons that made sense to people. Corrie ten Boom had no time for theological "angel-counting" or disputes. Corrie insisted her task was to point people to Christ. At eighty-six she told Pam Rosewell, "I must tell the people that they can come to the Lord Jesus as they are."

She never lost an opportunity. To a skycap, a pilot, a whatever, her natural question was "Do you know Jesus?"

Corrie made forgiveness a reality for many people.
Forgiveness was not a doctrine to Corrie ten Boom; it was a reality. This point was so vivid in Corrie's life, teaching, and preaching. She prayed for the man who set the trap that led to her family's arrest by the Gestapo. Before she wrote him, Corrie wrestled with a surge of hatred. After all, because of one man she had lost a father, a sister, and a brother, but Matthew 6:14, 15 came to her mind, "For if you forgive men when they sin against you, your heavenly Father will also forgive you. But if you do not forgive men their sins, your Father will not forgive your sins" (NIV). Her commitment to Scripture caused her to forgive, when many of her countrymen would not. "What you meant to be harmful, God used for my good," she wrote to the man.[57]

That was done by the mail. Forgiveness in person came harder. Two years passed. Then one night she saw him. He had come to her talk and waited afterwards. Instantly, her mind was filled with horror: the shame of walking naked past this man; the cruelty of Ravensbruck. The former guard.

He stuck out his hand, "A fine message, Fraulein! How good it is to know, as you say, all our sins are at the bottom of the sea!"

At that moment, in Corrie's mind, a massive dredging operation was under way. Her heart was churning.

He admitted that he had been a guard, but he did not remember Corrie. Then he said, "I have become a Christian. I know that God has forgiven me for the cruel things

131

I did there, but I would like to hear it from your lips as well. Fraulein, will you forgive me?"

Hell hushed and stood on tiptoes for a better view of the conversation. Corrie realized that she could not forgive him. How could this man expect all those horrid memories to disappear? "It seemed hours as I wrestled with the most difficult thing I had ever had to do."

She felt the coldness in her heart. Having worked with so many prison camp survivors, she knew the consequences psychologically of not forgiving. "Jesus, help me! I can lift my hand. I can do that much. You supply the feeling.

"And so woodenly, mechanically, I thrust my hand into the one stretched out to me. As I did, an incredible thing took place. The current started in my shoulders, raced down my arm, sprang into our joined hands. And then this healing warmth seemed to flood my whole being bringing tears to my eyes.

"I forgive you, brother!" she cried. "With all my heart."[58]

Forgiveness, she taught and lived, was not an emotion but a decision. Later in her ministry, after teaching from her experience for three decades, she declared, "It is an immutable law of God that man finds peace once when he is continually ready to forgive."[59]

Corrie taught that God had buried our sins in the deepest sea and then posted a sign, "No fishing allowed."

Corrie ten Boom touched lives through personal counseling, through speaking, through her books, and through her films.

When *The Hiding Place* was premiered, it was shown in a local theatre. A college admissions officer—angry and bitter because he was going through a divorce—was in the area interviewing prospective students and bought a ticket for something to do to take his mind off his problems and loneliness.

The film changed his life. He realized that his life was not Ravensbruck and that forgiveness was a possibility. If Corrie ten Boom survived all that, surely he could survive this divorce.

Corrie's words, "There is no pit so deep but that His love does not go deeper," sent him out of that theatre with a new lease on life.

I was that man. Corrie ten Boom touched me.

7.

Eartha Mary Magdalene White

BORN: November 8, 1876

PROFESSION: Social Worker

DIED: January 18, 1975

The motto on the laundry truck turned people's heads: "Put Your Duds in Our Suds!" And Eartha M. M. White, president of the Service Laundry Company, had her own slogan, "We wash everything but a dirty conscience." This black woman infused every project she tackled with equal zeal. When there was no one else to do it, Eartha volunteered.

Shortly before Eartha was born, a cousin came to visit Clara White, who'd already lost 12 children. The cousin announced, "Clara, I want you to name your child after the earth, that she might be a storehouse to the people."

Clara White was annoyed. "How do you know I'm going to have a child, or that it will be a girl? You're always meddling in other folks' affairs."

Clara's father, on the other hand, wanted the child named Mary Magdalene because "she chose the better part." So the names were combined: Eartha Mary Magdalene White was born in November 1876, just a few blocks from where her grandmother had been sold as a slave— for one thousand dollars.

When Eartha was young, all the neighborhood children came to her house for Christmas. Her mother was always prepared for them, having bought them small trinkets. But the children were sure that Santa had delivered the gifts. Even Eartha didn't suspect that her mother was the giver.

Converted as a child, Eartha was strongly influenced by her mother's benevolence. Even though she worked as a maid for the prominent Rollins family, she always had the time and energy to help those who were in distress. And that description eventually became characteristic of Eartha as well.

At the time of Eartha's birth, Jacksonville had been considered the "most liberal town in the South" concerning race relations. Levy, in his biography of Negro poet James Weldon Johnson, observed "a black man in Jacksonville had a better chance than anywhere else in the South of being treated on the basis of individual merit."[1] In fact, one New York leader said, "Jacksonville offered more opportunity for an ambitious Negro than any other American city." Eartha, with no lack of ambition, had been born in a city perfectly suited to her. By 1890, blacks composed 57 percent of the population.

Eartha attended Cookman Institute in Jacksonville and then moved to New York City, where she attended a fashionable finishing school for young women. She studied voice at Madame Thurber's National Conservatory of Music and joined the Oriental Opera Company. The company had been founded by a Mr. Graft, a millionaire who wanted to prove that blacks could sing opera as well as folk songs!

In 1896, she returned to Jacksonville, fell in love, and agreed to marry James Lloyd Johnson of South Carolina. When he died in June, a month before they were to marry, Eartha buried herself in her studies at the Florida Baptist Academy. At the turn of the century it was considered a point of honor not to marry if one's fiancé had died.

In her nineties, Eartha laughed, "I never married—I was too busy. What man would put up with me running around all the way I do!"

Indeed, the busier she became, the more she seemed to threaten men. Eventually the *Florida Times-Union* observed "Perhaps because female leadership in their race was sparse, the woman who had the spirit to grab the reins worked with exhausting vitality and versatility."[2] What man could keep up with her?

In 1889 she secured a teaching position in Bayard, convincing a local resident to give two lots on which to build a school. Under her influence it grew from 56 pupils to 240, but, not being afraid of hard work, she also moonlighted at the Afro American Insurance Company. Her boss got an insight into Eartha's character when a fire swept Jacksonville, destroying 466 acres, 146 city blocks, 2,368 buildings; 8,677 people were homeless. The company president, J. M. Walden, thought all was lost for the fledgling black insurance company. But he hadn't counted on Eartha's quick thinking: she had hired a wagon for two dollars and hauled the company's records to safety.[3]

Teaching school never completely held Eartha's interest, as too many needs in the black community needed her attention. After the yellow fever epidemic in 1888, the racial attitudes of the city leaders had turned sour. A new city government had enacted "Jim Crow" laws, forcing segregation. By 1901, the streetcars were segregated, and a spunky Eartha vowed never to ride them again. If she couldn't get a ride in a car, she walked. This editorial in the *Florida Times-Union* summarizes the racial attitude of many:

> Everything in the negro of which he possesses, of which he is proud has come to him from the white man. Everything of which he is ashamed is derived from his black ancestry . . . far better for him to take what he knows and go back to Africa.[4]

Eartha worked to overcome such bigotry. Because she wanted to maintain a spirit of cooperation between races, she worked through some of Jacksonville's leading white citizens to ameliorate the effects of the Jim Crow laws. When the Heard National Bank segregated its elevators, she wrote a stern letter: "Colored people are large depositors and will not continue as depositors in any bank that will so discriminate against them."[5]

In 1904, she developed a playground and used her own funds to hire a director after she convinced the city to donate the land. She used considerable effort and ingenuity to win their support. That year she gave up teaching to open a department store. She often got up at dawn to go down to the docks to buy inexpensive vegetables that she could resell to even her poorest customers. She sold her store in 1913 for $10,000 and then started a janitorial contracting service as well as a real estate office.

During this time she opened a home for the elderly. In an era before social security, blacks who had worked as maids, housemen, and cooks were often left destitute in old age. When one man wrote of a maid, "Her services have become valueless and I can no longer afford to take care of her," Eartha found a place for her. Others followed. V. C. Johnson, owner of the Dinsmore Dairy, gave her milk left over at the end of his daily routes. At harvest, Eartha often took the old people to pick surplus grapes. (Making a little wine, however, annoyed some of her supporters.)[6]

Eartha always had a good perspective on her singleness. In 1910, a Mrs. J. E. Young became incensed because Eartha sent a note to her husband requesting him to come to a quartet rehearsal. She snarled, "If you and I should live until the trumpet sounds, don't you ever send someone here with a message to my husband. Get one of your own."[7]

Eartha retorted, "Many thanks for your advice as to getting a husband of my own. That is not an easy thing to do, matter of fact, husbands are few and far between. When I am ready to marry, there is one in store for me without giving you any trouble." Then Eartha went on to dispel the reflection on her ministry cast by the woman. "I hope you will always observe the Second Commandment. As for casting reflections on my charity work, that is God's work. And He will take care of that!"[8]

When World War I broke out, Eartha kept a watchful eye on the blacks who served their country. Florida's Governor Craft initially requested that blacks not be included in the first draft, and later expressed outrage that blacks and whites had to strip for physical examinations in the same room. At the same time blacks were contributing $300,000 in the Liberty Bond Drive and dying for America's freedom.

Eartha became Director of War Camp Community Services—a organization designed to be a liaison between soldiers and civilians. As part of her assignment, she coordinated recreation for black soldiers in Savannah, Georgia. Moreover, she was the only Negro to attend President Wilson's Council on National Defense at the White House. Her presence at the meeting notified blacks that it was their war too! She was actively involved in helping blacks buy $300,000 in war bonds.[9]

It is difficult to understand how one woman could be in so many places at the same time. Yet if a need became evident to Eartha and if no one else volunteered, she added it to her already busy schedule. She daily rushed from project to project. Fortunately, she joked, she needed only a couple of hours of sleep per night. Her response to advice that she slow down was "The Master has need of us in other fields."

Often she got projects launched and managed them until other resources could be enlisted. For example, she started day care centers and raised the money to run them, then, when federal funds became available, she turned them over to the city of Jacksonville.

Those from whom she sought funds knew that if Eartha was involved the project was worthy of their support. She once said, "I have so many things to get done that I really should be a dozen people." Many nights she slept in her office rather than going home.[10]

After the War, she turned her attention to founding a home for tuberculosis patients. Why? Because she'd seen a need. One day in a vacant car barn, she'd found a man holding a cup of beans. Because of his rattling cough, he had been refused a hospital bed. Eartha made a place for people like him to die with clean sheets and dignity.

She also had an interest in politics and was a loyal Republican. When women gained the right to vote, Eartha urged women, white and black, to register and take advantage of the new opportunity and power. Democratic Judge John Dodge pleaded with white women to vote to repay the white men of the South for fifty years of protection from the "unmorality, savagery and beastly characteristics of the inherently vicious black man." Eartha could have protested his racist comments, but she held her peace and plotted. When long lines of black women stood in the hot sun waiting to register, chauvinistic offices deliberately responded with harassment and delay to discourage them. Eartha showed up with buckets of lemonade to make their waiting more pleasant. "Stay in line," she encouraged them. The Republican Party later praised her efforts which "produced marvelous results" in the female voter turnout.[11] Many of those women voted Republican in the next election.

Always looking for a cause, Eartha next organized the Clara White Mission, named, obviously, for her mother. People with any kind of need, of any race, could come to the mission and know they would not be turned away. Long before the United Way was established, she went door to door with a basket, begging for clothes, food, and fuel. She later commented, "When my own people didn't stand with me, God and my friends—particularly among my white friends—did." She was never ashamed to beg.[12]

She found a facility suitable for her mission operations. It had been a theater, a market, most recently a gambling hall, and Eartha knew it was large enough to accommodate her needs. She offered $150 a month rent, but she did not have the $300 it would take to fix it up. What did she do? She went to Personal Finance Company and asked for a loan, which was approved contingent upon her husband's signature. "Being married only to Jesus and the cause of kingdom-building," Eartha could not comply, but said, "I want to tell you . . . that I have no husband; but I am doing a good work and will surely repay the loan if it is granted."[13] As collateral they took all her household goods and they asked for a cosigner. Eartha wasn't about to give up. A doctor and her pastor agreed to sign, but were rejected because they had no salary. Finally the janitor of the Bethel Baptist Church was accepted and the loan approved.

All through the twenties and the depressed thirties, the "Angel of Mercy," as she came to be called, reached out to the orphan, the homeless, the aged, the tubercular. Her mother, Clara, had been known as "the last resort and dumping grounds for all sorts of charity cases," and so it was with Eartha.

When the state supervisor of the Florida Home Society, which had been founded to "help every needy child in Florida," received an application for a black child, he responded by saying that "Our society does not help any colored children at all." But he then suggested that the party might contact Eartha, whose arms were stretched a little wider. Children were important to her, so she launched a "Save 1,000 Boys from Juvenile Court" effort, saying that there had long been "a need in this city to take up the excess energy of healthy children." Eventually she got an appropriation of land from the city but only after considerable effort, energy, and ingenuity. She hired the first director, a Miss Cotter, out of her own funds.[14]

Few people could ever say no to Eartha White.

Nor could she say no to people in need. During the Depression she took a wagon downtown in front of Woolworth's, asked local singers to sing, and passed the hat among the crowds. As the Depression deepened, the city of Jacksonville even paid salaries for two cooks on Eartha's soup lines. In just five months of 1933, she fed 12,289 families.[15]

Eartha also took a personal interest in prisoners, feeling they were generally victims of unfortunate circumstances. For fifty years she taught Sunday school classes at the Duval County prison and worked to improve conditions. Her first jail pass read, "Please permit Miss White and associates to visit the camp to see the colored convicts as missionaries." Weekly she visited the King Edward Cigar factory to beg, "Give me some cigars for the boys in prison."

After release, both white and black men looked to her for guidance and assistance, but when some of the white men stayed overnight in her mission, the city officials complained. Eartha seemed to pay no attention to them, responding, "When a man is hungry, if he needs clothes, white or black, I'm going to give it to him!"[16]

During World War II she worked with A. Philip Randolph to organize a march in Washington, and their protest against job discrimination led to Executive Order 8802, which banned racial discrimination in governmental service.

By the mid-1960s her influence was incredible. She sponsored the Eartha White Nursing Home, two boarding homes for the ambulatory, two child care centers, one lodging for alcoholics, and a mission to feed, clothe, and comfort the poor. But her joy was in the 120-bed nursing home opened in 1967.

In 1970, she was honored with the Lane Bryant Volunteer Award as *the* outstanding volunteer in America.

In her old age, her service was honored, twice at the White House. At age 95, she flew alone across the country to Anaheim to receive the Better Life Award from the American Nursing Home Association. However, the Lane Bryant Volunteer Award was the most prestigious. It was a one-time honor granted to the American "considered to have made the most significant contribution in his/her community."[17]

What Characterized the Unique Ministry of Eartha White?

Her faith. Eartha explained her commitment on the basis of her relationship with God: "I live by John 15:7, 'If ye abide in me, and my words abide in you, ye shall ask what ye will. . . .' That is a contract with God. I try to fill my side of the contract: He fulfills His."

At the Plaza Hotel she called a press conference after receiving the Lane Bryant award. She urged reporters to tell the nation: "To get out of yourselves and let God use you. He has the solution to *all* of our problems." Her comment then doesn't seem far removed from what she wrote in 1910: "God has worked wonderfully with me. He has miraculously taken care of me and He is going to continue to do so."[18]

Her faith gave her the courage to love and give whole-heartedly everything God had given her.

Her sense of debt. Her desire to work was shaped by her philosophy of work: "The main trouble with the world is that its inhabitants don't take time to get out of themselves and wake up to the fact that nothing here on this earth belongs to them." To reporters in New York Eartha admitted, "Most of my life has been spent in service. You must not forget that the earth is the Lord's and the fullness thereof." Eartha spent her life repaying God for what He had given her, and she strongly felt that what she did for her fellow men and women she did for Jesus. One of her favorite poems was: "Lord, let this my motto be. That while I live for others, Lord, I live for Thee."

She said, "Service is the price you pay for the space you occupy." Eartha took seriously her commitment to "serve God and humanity."[19]

When asked what she would do with the money received as part of the Lane Bryant award she laughed. "I've already decided. I want it to serve humanity. The money is to God, not to me. What would I do with it? Sit around the Plaza Hotel? I'm too busy."[20]

By this time, Eartha had turned her house into a museum of Negro history and moved into a small room at the Mission. Even her home was given back to the people she served.

Her vision. Eartha White believed that she could make a difference. Although she mastered governmental bureaucracy and red tape, she still had time for the common person. Her correspondence shows that people felt free to write Eartha about their problems—even about a simple blood test being lost.

Samuel J. Tucker once said that there were three black institutions in Jacksonville: Edward Waters College, the Urban League, and Miss White.[21] Her philosophy of life was summed up in a simple statement: "Do all the good you can for all the people you can." Indeed, even her birthdays became a means of expanding her work. In her later years, her birthday celebrations grew so large that they had to be held in the Jacksonville Civic Center. Thousands attended, and gifts, often monetary, were redirected to her organizations. By 1970 the *Florida Times-Union* had titled her "the Ambassador of Concern."

As she grew older, many people grew concerned about Eartha. When one reporter asked her when she would retire, she answered, "Retire? No, no—that's not for me. I'll never retire. That's just for rich people."[22]

Much of her vision centered around helping the Negro race, and what an irony for Eartha to discover eventually that her father had been white. When Clara White applied for a widow's military pension in 1881 the army launched a full investigation because of rumors about Eartha's light skin. A Dr. Fernandez admitted that Eartha's father was a member of one of Jacksonville's most prominent white families, although the name of the father was never revealed to prevent a major scandal.

Eartha spent her life helping anyone who needed her, realizing that "When the world was created, there were no blacks or whites, just people! We have equally fought and we have killed thousands of people with our selfishness and greed."[23]

Eartha worked fifty years in her missions programs without compensation. Yet each day she dared dream of her "hope for a bright future when there is no black or white, nor north or south." Each day offered her the possibility to "do all the good you can, for all the people you can."

Before her death, she wrote:

I can well remember when we worked out in the cornfields and once in a while we would steal away to Jesus. Steal away to a quiet place where we could pray. That was only yesterday. *Today* we must live as God's mouthpiece and prove to Him that He can depend on us.[24]

Eartha White, a single adult who made a difference, died on January 18, 1975. Heaven gained an angel and Jacksonville lost a legend.

8.

Luther Rice

BORN: March 25, 1783

PROFESSION: Minister-Missionary-Agent

DIED: September 25, 1836

Luther Rice was obsessed with the work to which he'd given his life. During his last days, his brainchild, Columbian College in Washington, D.C., filled his thoughts. After one of Luther's strokes, a physician asked him if he were ready to die. "Yes," he said, "though I should like to bring up the college first." He proceeded to solicit a donation from the doctor—in essence a double donation because Luther had no way to pay him.

Rice had dreamed a great vision—to mold American Baptists into a national denomination. He worked to fulfill that dream by dedicating his life to the cause of education and world evangelization.

In New England families, the youngest boy had a particular function: to stay on the farm and care for his parents as they aged. Luther Rice's father had done that for Luther's grandfather. But Luther didn't. The first of his many alienations came with his family.

Luther Rice grew up in an era profoundly impacted by the Great Awakening, exemplified by the Calvinist preaching of Jonathan Edwards. Luther grappled with an acute consciousness of his sin as opposed to God's holiness. Rice even questioned the possibility of his sin being forgiven, and he lived in fear of eternal judgment.[1]

At age sixteen, Luther and a group of friends, without the permission of their parents, went off to Georgia to work in the logging business. Although gone only six months, his parents worried that the venture had introduced him to certain "undesirable" individuals. But the trip seemed to have a good effect. When he returned, he was even more concerned with religious matters. From his seventeenth to nineteenth years, he wrestled in a complex spiritual battle, being tormented with hellish fears.[2]

He spoke of his plight to his mother, who referred him to their pastor, Mr. Whitney, an opinionated but highly composed man. (As he preached one day, someone handed him a note, "Your house is on fire!" He continued preaching, and by the end of the service the house had burned to the ground.)[3] Whitney had difficulty comprehending the depth of Luther's guilt and struggle. He proposed that Luther join the church in the manner of the Half-Way Covenanters: "I've done my part, God, now do Yours." So on March 14, 1802, Rice was accepted as a member, yet he still had no sense of peace.

He religiously read Richard Baxter's *Call of the Unconverted* and *Saint's Rest;* Doddridge's *Rise and Progress of Religion in the Soul;* and John Newton's *Works,* heavy stuff for a teenager.[4]

One year later, Rice still struggled, and he determined to do everything he could to earn his salvation.

> During those months of subjective probing, Luther tried to analyze his own heart and its condition. His keen conscience about his guilt led him to lacerate his own soul in attempts at true penitence. The self-castigation often approached morbidity. He vowed to sit up all night and petition for salvation; he resolved to drive under every desire of his body; to fast, to refrain from any levity or frivolity. There raged a perpetual battle between the spirit and the flesh.[5]

For example, in 1803, his father's sister visited the farm. Aunt Rebecca asked her nephew to loan her twelve and a half cents to buy snuff. Afterwards, Luther was devastated that he had complied, "because I was grieved to see her so bewitched by such a habit!"

The winter of 1804, Luther trudged through the snow to visit the Reverend J. Robinson, a strict Calvinist and relative through marriage. Robinson urged Rice to act upon the scriptural commands, to ignore his own doubts, and to have faith in God's provision.[6]

In that era, many pastors suggested that someone considering conversion answer the following question: Would you be willing to give God a sheet of paper that was blank except for your name and allow Him "to fill up your destiny as might seem good in His sight?"

On Saturday, September 14, 1805, a spiritual crisis engulfed Rice and

> I felt that I should be willing thus to put a blank into the hand of God, to be by Him filled as He might please; Nay, being weary of the quarrel with God, so to speak, in which I had been so long involved, I felt as if I could wish it were literally a fact. . . . And I then found in this disposition of absolute unreserved submission to the will of God, a sweet and blessed tranquility.[7]

Even his family recognized a decisive change the next morning at breakfast. Released from the burden of his sin, he later recalled, "That Sabbath was truly a delightful one to me. I now felt perfectly well as to health, and was continually singing by myself, instead of weeping and wailing as before."

Rice wanted to get more education, and to earn money he got a teaching job in nearby Paxton. For a brief time he boarded with families, taught school children in the mornings, and led a "singing school" at night. He then enrolled in Leicester Academy, known for its strength in Latin. Although the classrooms were in a ramshackle building, Luther enjoyed the challenge. The next summer, Luther worked for his father and became concerned with the anemic spiritual climate of his church. He started prayer meetings, which the pastor immediately disapproved of. Pastor Whitney had not understood Luther's burden with sin and guilt, and he showed little tolerance for Luther's criticism and analysis.[8]

Knowing how the pastor felt, Rice's neighbors were reluctant to offer their homes for the prayer meetings.

Finally Asaph Rice—Luther's older brother—offered his home, although he did not participate in the sessions. Despite a fifteen-year age difference, the gesture sealed a lifelong friendship between the two brothers. Later, Asaph bought land from Luther and helped him finance his college education.

Although most of Rice's peers chose Harvard, Luther chose Williams, apparently because of the low tuition and because of its spiritual climate. Luther hadn't been at school long before he wrote home to Asaph, "I have deliberately made up my mind to preach the gospel to the heathen, and I do not know but it may be Asia."[9]

By the fall of 1808, a prayer group—which had originally met under a haystack—evolved into a fledgling missionary group. Rice and four others who became known as "the Brethren" signed a pledge "to effect a mission to the world's teeming in foreign lands." Previous to this time, Evelyn Thompson, Luther's biographer, noted, there had been groups committed to promoting missions, praying and sending, but "the Brethren set itself to the task of *going*, in the person of its members, to foreign lands."[10]

New members of the group had to be interviewed by two members who "weighed the candidate's character, situation and ability to bear an assignment." Many were rejected.

> At first they felt no candidate who was engaged or planned to marry should be admitted. Each man must keep himself in readiness to go *at any time* the Brethren designated him.[11]

The group conducted their business by using oaths, secrecy, and coded records. They gathered every Sunday at sunrise to pray for missions; they often read letters and reports from the London Mission Society and reprinted missionary sermons. Slowly, they attracted pastors to their cause.

In 1809, the group graduated from Williams and they all entered Andover Theological Seminary, where they enlisted the support of Adoniram Judson from Brown, Samuel Newell from Harvard, and Samuel Nott from Union College. Luther was elected president when the group was renamed "Society of Inquiry on the Subject of Missions."

As seminary graduation neared, they revealed to various professors their intentions to volunteer for mission service. Around the same time a convention of Congregational ministers met at nearby Bradford, Massachusetts. The Society quickly drafted a petition asking for the convention's support and blessing. The plan was adopted, resulting in the formation of the American Board of Commissioners for Foreign Missions; Judson, Newell, Nott, and Gordon Hall were designated as its first missionary candidates. Over the next two years, the Board corresponded with the London Missionary Society about accepting the young unmarried men, who wished "to serve the Savior in a heathen land." At first the Commissioners proposed a joint venture, but the British insisted that, if they financed the operation, the missionaries be under their supervision. The Americans would not agree to such an arrangement.

Because the British venture fell through, financial problems delayed the sending of any of the men. Although the Commissioners had received a bequest from the widow of John Norris for $30,000, the family contested the will. The

Commissioners only had $500 in cash and at least $6,000 was needed to send out the team of missionaries.[12]

Rice was excluded from the first round of appointments for three reasons: He had not finished seminary, there was a lack of cash, and he had not resolved his relationship with Rebecca Eaton, to whom he had proposed marriage— but *without* revealing his commitment to missions.

Luther saw things differently. His mind was set on going. He pleaded with the Commissioners to appoint him, and one Commissioner, Mr. Worchester, took Luther's side. Cautiously, the Board agreed to sponsor Rice *if* he raised his own money.

When the Board learned that the ship *Harmony* would sail for India in mid-February, they decided immediately to ordain Rice and the other candidates.

Within just six days Luther Rice begged enough money to finance his passage to India. On February 6, 1812, in the Old Tabernacle Meeting House, Salem, a council examined the candidates on their motives and faith and gave them several directives: First, to abstain "scrupulously" from meddling with political concerns, especially since another war with England loomed; second, upon arrival on the field they were to organize a mission and elect a secretary and treasurer; third, they were to organize a church and to "treat converts with charity and caution." Furthermore, the men were ordered to admit to their churches only those who showed evidence of their regeneration.[13]

The tabernacle was packed for this historic moment. People came by wagon and horseback; many walked. Dr. Lenoe Woods, a professor at Andover, preached the ordination sermon. "Are you not resolved to do everything, to part with everything, to submit to everything, to forward this glorious design of filling the earth with the knowledge of the Lord?"

Then he turned to the audience, "Think of how it will be in Asia a century or two from hence" because of the influence of these men. He probably had no idea how prophetic his words were.[14]

The Commissioners had booked the missionaries on two ships so that one party would survive if disaster struck. Rice and his party sailed from Philadelphia on February 18, but because of wind conditions they reached Calcutta six weeks after Judson and Newell.

By this time the United States and England were at war; an embargo was on and sailing was dangerous. The long voyage had, however, given Rice a chance to visit with Rev. William Johns, an English Baptist. After one session—a spirited exchange on water baptism—Rice wrote in his journal, "I wish he [Johns] would reason candidly and not rest conclusions upon his bare assertions."

Johns and another missionary, a Mr. Lawson, shared some books with Luther, one of which contained a treatise on baptism and struck a responsive chord in Rice. Later, he wrote, "May the Lord guide us in the way of truth for His name's sake." Daily the men argued their traditions: Rice defended infant baptism as a parallel to circumcision among the Israelites. Johns dogmatically insisted on adult immersion.[15]

When Luther reached Calcutta, he discovered that Judson had altered his views on baptism, which had previously been similar to Luther's. Rice challenged him, but Adoniram Judson and his wife, Ann, were baptized on September 6, 1812, and Rice listened closely to Judson's first sermon on baptism, based on the text, "Go ye therefore, and teach all nations, *baptizing them*" (Matthew

28:19). In his diary, Rice confessed that he was wavering on the subject, and two months later Rice himself was baptized. He wrote his parents, "Yesterday, I was baptized by the Rev. Mr. Wade . . . it was a comfortable day in my soul."[16]

But that comfort did not last long. He and Judson faced an ethical dilemma. Congregationalists had sent them to India, and the two missionaries seemed to have three choices: to turn back on their missionary efforts, to align with the English missionaries, or to attempt to solicit the financial support of American Baptists.

Although some of the English Baptists seemed willing to take on the Americans, William Carey encouraged Judson and Rice to enlist the support of American Baptists. Two other circumstances finally influenced Rice's decision. He became ill with liver·inflammation, and the East India Company did not want American missionaries working in their territory. So when Rice was deported to the Isle of France, he decided to return home to America to explain his situation to the Commissioners.[17]

His thirtieth birthday was spent aboard the *Donna Maria* sailing for Saint Salvador, where he hoped to find a ship bound for America. He prayed, "I renewedly give myself to the Lord; renewedly devote myself to the cause of missions and beg God to accept me as His, and to the missionary cause; and allow me, if it may be Thy will, a few years to labour in the missionary field, and then receive me to heaven, for Christ's sake."[18]

Rice arrived in New York on September 7, 1812, and he began earnest preparation for his meeting. On the fifteenth, he faced a hostile, annoyed board who met him coldly, and refused to give him a direct official statement of their attitude toward him. Rice found out by inquiry that the Board regard the very fact of his conversion to Baptist views and his immersion in itself a severance of the connection with the society that had commissioned him. The Board found it hard to treat Judson and Rice with Christian courtesy and fraternal regard.[19]

Eventually some critics accused Rice of mercenary motives. The Baptists, however, greeted Rice with open arms and he set out as an itinerant preacher to enlist Baptist support. Traveling from town to town, he spoke wherever he could gather a group of Baptists.

On April 10, 1814, Rice addressed Congress on his work. As Luther's influence increased, he urged the formation of the General Missionary Convention of the Baptist Denomination in the United States of America. Because the group would meet every three years, it became known as the Triennial Convention. Although this particular convention would eventually dissolve over the slavery issue, it was the forerunner of the Southern Baptist Convention. Between conventions, business matters were to be administered by commissioners or what became the Baptist Board of Foreign Missions for the United States. Rice served as its agent, or official representative, and the board promptly passed a resolution praising the "beloved brother" for his "zealous. . . . and faithful services." It urged him to

continue his itinerant services in these United States for a reasonable time, with a view to excite the public mind more generally, to engage in missionary exertion; and to assist in originating societies or Institutions, for carrying the missionary design into execution.[20]

The Board voted to accept Judson as their missionary and to pay his support. Rice reported raising $1,836.67 on his recent tour ($345 of which was collected in Presbyterian churches), and for the next three years he spread the word across the country—that missions were important and that they needed money.[21]

From 1814 to 1817, Rice traveled the American countryside, particularly the Southern states, either on a horse or by buggy. He often traveled by night and usually alone. Road conditions were such that he sometimes forged his own path, yet he admitted that fear was not a companion of his.

In the fall of 1814, Luther saw Rebecca Eaton, whom he had never forgotten. Indeed, when he'd been in India, Ann Judson had written urgent letters to Rebecca, asking that she come to Calcutta as soon as possible. When Luther had come back to the States, the Judsons expected him to return within months—with a wife. But then and now, in 1814, Rebecca's answer remained no.[22]

The Board of Foreign Missions frequently and candidly discussed Rice's commitment to returning to the field, but if he were to return they felt he should have a wife at his side. Yet the Board had to face another issue: if Luther married and returned to the field, who would replace him in raising money? The Board recognized that Rice's itinerant preaching and fund raising were very successful. On July 19, 1816, he had traveled 6,600 miles and had collected almost $4,000.[23]

Although his primary thrust was missionary, Luther quickly perceived the need for an educated clergy. Many of the ministers he met were self-taught. Although they were deeply devoted to their work, their logic and homiletic technique was grossly inadequate for the tasks ahead of them.

Because of the lack of theological training, because of the lack of communication systems and channels, Baptists held a wide variety of beliefs. Luther's desire for trained missionaries placed him in direct confrontation with the antimissionaries who opposed Sunday schools, temperance societies, theological training, a paid clergy, and mission boards. By 1820, individual churches and state associations were voting *not* to support missions. Some Baptist churches were expelled from state associations for defending the work of mission boards.[24]

How could anyone oppose missions? First, the opponents countered that missionary-sending agencies were contrary to the Bible, which sanctions only the local church. Second, strict Calvinists argued that God didn't need human help to effect the salvation of the elect and that the nonelect were predestined to be damned. Third, the movement objected to the centralization of power that a missionary society would bring about. Additionally, the frontiersman was suspicious of an educated and paid clergy, and, finally, opponents spread the word that churches would be "taxed" to support missions.[25]

Rice met hostile resistance to his dream but he ignored the sensational charges made against him and continued to yearn for a college where ministers might trade "their loud oratory for skilled interpretation of the Bible." Rice argued that the denomination's future depended on the leaders and how well they were trained. He eventually saw that starting a university would be the most beneficial thing he could do for the denomination.

In 1820, the Triennial Convention approved the idea of a school. Senator Henry Clay of Kentucky helped win congressional support for a charter, so the school, Columbian College, could be located in Washington, D.C.

Eventually, his "dreamchild" led to Luther's undoing. Always a dreamer rather than an administrator, Luther's college work took too much time from his mission assignment; he allowed construction to proceed before he had cash; he allowed numbers of "preacher boys" to attend without paying tuition. By 1823, the college was heavily in debt. Luther's mission work was suffering because he was working so hard for the school.[26]

The philosophical debates also continued to flare up, and criticism of Luther grew. Through all the charges Rice refused to debate any opponent. His critics did, however, successfully tarnish his reputation. Although his campaign to raise pledges for new buildings at Columbian had gone well, many pledges went uncollected. As a result, Rice was forced to stay close to Washington to deal with the financial crisis and he lost contact with many of his supporters.

In September 1825, an investigative committee recommended Luther's dismissal as the college's official representative. Although there were serious allegations about his misuse of money, none were proved, although he did admit that his bookkeeping skills were poor.

In May 1826, the Triennial Convention decided that their commitment should be solely to missions. Because they needed someone who was dedicated to their cause, they stripped Luther of his responsibilities. Although he now had no sponsor or salary, he personally carried on with his dream. He wrote, "I have no private property but while the college owes one cent, or any person is bound to pay anything for it . . . leave me and the debts yoked together."[27]

For the rest of his life, Luther traveled, preaching, raising money, and often begging for money to reduce the debts of Columbian College. He spent his small inheritance and then paid for his expenses by selling his books and by depending on his friends.

While he worked for a national Baptist institution, in actuality, Luther fostered the development of almost one hundred Baptist colleges and schools.

During a tour of the South, although raising money for Columbian, he made such an impassioned speech on the value of Christian education that a group of men formed Kentucky's Georgetown College. Rice was also influential in the founding of such colleges as Colby (1820); Newton Theological Seminary (1825); Furman (1827); University of Richmond (1832); Wake Forest (1827); and Denison (1832).

Although the Baptists formally had turned their backs on Columbian College, Rice could not. Indeed, another man might have accepted any of the college presidencies he was offered—Transylvania, Georgetown College, University of Kentucky. He kept traveling, preaching, pleading, raising money—even when he should have been in bed. Bed? Whose? After 1826, he did not even own a bed but relied on the hospitality of farmers and planters. He carried the Baptist cause into small meeting houses in out-of-the-way hamlets but also to the hearthstones and tables of laymen, where he always seemed a welcome visitor. If he hadn't won his way into the hearts of the church bureaucracy, he had into the hearts of the people.

He was jovial and friendly and brought life to the homes he entered.[28]

Rice frequently stayed in the homes of Colonel John Pollard and his neighbor John Bagby in Virginia. Pollard sent four sons and Bagby five to Columbian; of the nine, six became ministers.[29]

On a visit to Caroline County, Virginia, Rice became ill while at church and could not even drive his buggy to the home of his host, Samuel Redd. Mrs. Redd reported:

> He was very sick for a week or 10 days. When his clothes were brought in by the washerwoman, they were examined and put in order—a thing very much needed. He spent little on himself. All that could be saved must go to the college. There were among the clothes a cravat so worn it was past mending which I thought no robbery to appropriate, and put in its place—new, and as much alike as it could be, even to the small "L.R." embroidered on it.[30]

In late age, Luther apparently courted a widow who had three grown sons. He wrote the college, "It is my intention to marry, and I must needs have a home." Rice wanted to live in one of the houses owned by Columbian, but for one reason or another Luther never married her. "Tradition has it that the *rich* widow was fearful her inheritance would find its way into the treasury of Columbian College, her love of the College being considerably less than Rice's."[31]

On January 1, 1836, Rice made a New Year's resolution: to read the Bible through systematically that year—five chapters on Sabbath, three every other day.

The Lord in His mercy, has brought me to the beginning of another year. I think I have made some little progress in religion the past year, but far less than I thought. God grant I may do better, should life be preserved through this year also.[32]

But Luther did not live through the year. In September he died in the home of a friend, Dr. R. G. Mays. Two days before Luther's death, Mays asked him if he had any pressing instructions. "Send my sulky, my horse and baggage to Brother Brooks, with directions to send them to Brother Sherwood, and say that they all belong to the College."[33]

What a life! What a commitment!

What Characterized the Unique Ministry of Luther Rice?

His networking abilities. Luther was always looking for contacts. When the first Triennial Convention assembled, only Rice knew every person in attendance. Edward Pollard, a historian, noted that "a man's life is measurably the multiplicity of his contacts." For a man whose address was his saddle, Luther had developed an incredible network; some of the people he got to support his work went on to be well-known and influential.[34] Thompson commented on Rice's gift:

Since he felt men were the key to any new venture, he was always seeking them—committed men of ability and dedication, men willing to build for the future. He recruited many who led the denomination for the next half century. And though in time his enemies may have formed a sizable regiment, the men he enlisted have supplied the outposts in each of the denomination's new undertakings.[35]

His "connecting" didn't come without some effort on his part. He spent an hour or two every day corresponding with persons in all parts of the country: students, missionaries, pastors, or thank-you letters to those who had contributed. Generally, he wrote ten to twenty letters per night, after his host went to bed.

His ability to encourage and train. Whether on horseback or at the college, Luther encouraged and trained a generation of leaders. A number of young men at Columbian College became part of that "brilliant army" of leadership among the Baptists. Many would not have had the chance to attend college without Rice's encouragement. One recalled:

> When I was a boy of 16, living in Connecticut, and with no means of defraying the expenses of my education, a letter came to my pastor from the Rev. Luther Rice saying, "Tell the young man to come to Columbian College, Washington City, and I reckon we shall be able to put him through." I accordingly went to Washington, and found Mr. Rice a warm friend and ready to aid me in the severe struggle with poverty through which I then and in subsequent years passed, in preparing for the Christian ministry.[36]

One of the charges against Rice was that he let too many such young men attend Columbian on tuition "waivers." Clearly his generosity paid handsome rewards in leadership.

One of the most influential people Rice knew and trained was John Mason Peck, called "the Father of the American Baptist Home Mission Board," who served as a missionary in the Missouri Territory. Rice also recruited Jonathan Wade, Eugene Kincaid, and George Hough to assist Judson, who was serving in Burma.

Luther's charity toward others even reached to his enemies. He did not answer any of his critics; nor did he attack other denominations. He felt his brethren should love one another as Jesus demanded.

His prayer life. Rice prayed seven times a day: midnight, daybreak, before breakfast (if with a family), noon, twilight, after supper (if with a family), just before bed. He fasted the first and third Mondays of the month. He also divided the prayer periods to focus on specific needs such as the college and revival in Washington. In his diary he reminded himself:

> Make it a point to pray for every family where I tarry a night, or call in the day, for every person individually who makes a contribution for any object for which I receive funds; for everyone I converse with in the day; for every person I see in the day, all as particularly as practicable.[37]

This course tends to keep religion alive in the soul. This practice itself should have shown his opponents that his heart was set on serving his God.

In the end, tiny Columbian College passed from Baptist control into private hands, but it thrives today as George

Washington University. Ultimately, many of those Baptist churches Rice so lovingly nourished became the backbone of the Southern Baptist Convention.

Luther's singleness greatly affected his contribution. If he'd had a wife, he may have quickly returned to India, where his influence may or may not have been great. If he'd had a wife and stayed in the States, he would not have been able to spend so much time on the road visiting churches, collecting money, and building the state associations.

One man—"alone" by today's standards—changed the course of American church history.

9.

Henrietta Mears

BORN: October 23, 1890

PROFESSION: Christian educator/publisher

DIED: March 22, 1961

It was a long way from Hollywood to the Taj Mahal in India, and Henrietta Mears was enjoying every moment of her well-earned vacation. The tour guide, in order to demonstrate the acoustics of the "wonder of the world," stepped up on a little platform and shouted: "There is no God but Allah, and Mohammed is his prophet!" His words rang through the hall.

Vacation or no, the challenge was too much for Miss Mears. "May I try that?" she asked. When the guide gave her permission, Henrietta Mears exclaimed in her powerful voice: "Jesus Christ, Son of God, is Lord over all!" Like a volley of rifle fire, her words echoed until she was satisfied that the tour could continue.[1] Every moment, even one that appeared accidental or coincidental, was an opportunity for ministry. That's what Henrietta Mears believed and taught and lived.

This was no ordinary tourist. Henrietta Mears not only loved colorful hats, she "wore" many hats: director of Christian Education at the First Presbyterian Church in Hollywood, California, founder and president of Gospel Light Publishing Company, founder and director of Forest Home Christian Conference Center, counselor, but most important "Teacher."

Henrietta was born in Fargo, North Dakota, into the home of a prominent banker. Her father exclaimed, "Praise God, it's a girl. I couldn't face rearing another son!" Henrietta, the baby of the family, adored by her siblings, was the apple of her father's eye. Her keen intelligence was recognized by her parents and encouraged. After one day at kindergarten, she announced to her parents, "Kindergarten is to 'muse little children, and I'se 'mused enough. I want to be edicated."

On Easter Sunday, 1895, Henrietta announced to her mother that she wanted to become a Christian and join the church. "Everyone will think you are too young to understand," her mother replied. Henrietta refused to accept that answer, so her mother agreed to talk to the pastor.

A few weeks later, Henrietta, age five, stood before the First Baptist Church in Minneapolis and answered the questions about faith so clearly that the congregation broke into laughter. Henrietta looked to her mother who reminded her that they were laughing with her, not at her.[2]

Mrs. Mears was a strong Christian worker in the local church. She often visited the Florence Crittenden Home for unwed mothers. When Henrietta was ten, she accompanied her mother and the visit had a profound impact on her life. When her mother fixed baskets for the poor at Christmas, she included Henrietta in the shopping. While the baskets contained staple goods, her mother added butter and jelly and extras. "The Lord doesn't just give dry bread you know, Henrietta. And we will put in milk and cream too, for the Lord always gives extra things."[3] The point would later shape Henrietta's philosophy of ministry: Extras produce excellence.

A freak childhood accident played a crucial role in spiritually shaping Henrietta Mears. When she accidentally stuck a hat pin into the pupil of her eye, physicians said there was nothing they could do. If God had made her eye, Henrietta reasoned, then God could heal it. She and her mother sent for a Mr. Ingersol from First Baptist who came and prayed for her.[4] Later, specialists were amazed that she could see; she lived out her lifetime with a hole in her left eye.

Henrietta next battled muscular rheumatism and became very weak. Again, she called for Mr. Ingersol. Again, she was healed. However, she became aware of a growing loss of her eyesight, a condition diagnosed as extreme myopia. Before she entered the University of Minnesota, her physician strenuously counseled against the decision. That much study and reading could further weaken the eye and lead to blindness.

"If," Henrietta responded, revealing a hint of skepticism with the prognosis, "I am going to be blind by thirty, then blind I shall be! But I want something in my brain to think about!"[5]

The reality caused her to discipline her study habits, to study by daylight rather than by electricity, to develop her concentration on lectures, and master a book in one reading. Her mother had had a habit of walking into a room where Henrietta was reading, grabbing the book away from her, and demanding, "What are you reading?" The habit developed Henrietta's gift of concentration.

Although Henrietta asked God to heal her, her eyesight became her "thorn in the flesh," a lifelong struggle. "Yet," she explained, "I believe my greatest spiritual asset throughout my entire life has been my failing sight, for it has kept me absolutely dependent upon God."[6]

After graduation, Henrietta taught high school chemistry (which prepared her for many hours of counseling with scientists and engineers who had difficulty reconciling faith and science). She organized a football team and became a devoted fan. Despite her busy academic schedule, she also stayed involved in Sunday school. At First Baptist, Henrietta was asked to take over a a class of eighteen-year-old girls who called themselves The Snobs and refused to admit newcomers.

Henrietta won their hearts. When the Sunday school was reorganized, Henrietta had a class of one, because so many of her pupils became involved in teaching Sunday school. So she and her sister, Margaret, canvassed the neighborhood for prospects. Fifty-five appeared the first Sunday; within five years the class had a membership of over five hundred.[7]

It was Henrietta and Margaret's custom to invite visiting ministers to Sunday dinner. So, Dr. Stewart MacLennan from the First Presbyterian Church of Hollywood, California, spent the afternoon with the two sisters. When

Henrietta offered to drive him back to the hotel to rest for the evening service, he said, "Do I have to go?"

Instead, he stayed and shared the outlines of a new series of sermons. At the end of the afternoon, MacLennan invited the two sisters to come out to California.

The pastor of First Baptist knew that Henrietta was wrestling with a call: to stay in public education, which would mean going to Columbia University for graduate work, or to go into full-time Christian service. He suggested that she get away to Europe. "It may give you a vision of this world that will determine the direction of your life."[8] The year was 1927, and it was to be the first of many trips.

After returning from Europe, the Mears sisters decided to visit MacLennan and were impressed with the scope of ministries at the church. Henrietta spoke to several of the groups, and soon Dr. MacLennan invited her to become director of Christian Education. "Out of the question," Henrietta answered. "I have a home, I have a teaching contract that I have to honor."

Once she returned to Minnesota, MacLennan wrote, telegraphed, and telephoned, asking her to reconsider. The First Presbyterian Church wanted her; she agreed to return to Hollywood for another look. One evening in a restaurant, she found herself saying, "If I were going to do such and such, I'd. . . ." Years later, she would counsel young adults struggling with a decision, "Look to the horizon. Do you see the slightest change? The slightest speck? If you do follow it." That advice came out of her own struggle.[9]

So, the Mears sisters moved to tinsel town, the city of make-believe, Hollywood.

At her first staff meeting she chose to be cautious. "I know what you are thinking, 'Another director of the Sunday school—new plans, new ideas, her way of doing things!' " Henrietta won her audience with the line, " 'What does she know about Hollywood, anyway?' "

"You don't like changes and neither do I. . . . So here is what I thought we might do: We'll all relax for six months and use the time for observation, and then we'll sit down and evaluate the situation and decide together what we need to do."

"What *we* need to do," the Mears philosophy of Christian leadership training, won their hearts. When the church needed painting, Henrietta took a brush and painted the women's rest room. Miss Mears would never ask her teachers to do something she was not prepared to do.[10]

Henrietta Mears was a great teacher. She invested tremendous hours in preparation. To her, *who* is doing the teaching, and the quality of *their* Christian experience, is as important as *what* is taught.[11]

However, there was the problem of curriculum. Sunday school literature for children was inadequate. While much of the literature was biblically sound (the one exception was a manual that said Paul had survived shipwreck by eating carrots), there were no pictures. Nor was there grading: The same book was used for the six-year-olds and the twelve-year-olds.

Moreover, Miss Mears could find little sequencing. One Sunday a child might study King Saul, the next Sunday, Saul of Tarsus, jumping around in the Bible, a method Miss Mears deplored as the "grasshopper" approach. In 1929 two conversations set her on a new path. One little boy told her, "I don't wanna go to Sunday school anymore. All they do is tell you the same story over and over and over again; only it gets dumber and dumber." The second experience shattered her. A brilliant young man asked, "What's wrong, Miss Mears? I've gone to Sunday school all my life, but if I had to take an examination on the Bible today, I'd flunk." What was true of these two was true of others, she realized. But she also knew that if the Bible is taught effectively and with enthusiasm, people will respond.[12]

With the pastor's permission—"Use anything you want as long as it teaches the Bible"—Henrietta swung into action. She designed a system to determine the expectations for each age level. Then she began writing the lessons for the entire junior department every week, staying a week or two ahead. Meanwhile, other departments needed her attention. The counseling needs intensified.

Miss Mears's secretary, Ethel May Baldwin, typed, mimeographed, and stapled the materials. Certainly, there were problems: mimeographing rubbed off on Sunday clothes. When Henrietta approached printers, they told her that the costs for publishing her materials would be prohibitive. Still, she continued writing, cutting pictures off old religious calendars.

Meanwhile, word of the effectiveness of her materials spread across Southern California. Teachers begged for copies. "Impossible," Miss Mears answered. Visitors to the church were always amazed at the children. What materials do you use? was a constant question. "Oh, just some mimeographed materials that some of us are writing and putting together," she'd reply. Then she met Marion Falconer, a druggist by trade and a Sunday school superintendent in a Presbyterian church in Anaheim. After observing the uniqueness of her program, he wanted the materials for his own church. Miss Mears gave him all the reasons why not but finally promised, "I'll look into the matter of printing once again."

Within months she found a printer who delayed payment until the books were sold. Cary Griffin sat on her couch and educated her on the realities of printing. The system required Mears and her staff to write nine books a quarter. However, she made a helpful decision: not to date the materials, making them reusable.

The result was the start of Gospel Light Publishing Company. One of her teachers asked, "Who is going to ship these books and take care of the accounting?" Stanley Eagle's garage soon became their first warehouse. When Esther Ellinghusen, one of Mears's colleagues wrote a check for $84.74 to pay for the engravings of the junior pupils' book, her mother griped, "That's money down the drain!"[13]

Although it was during the Depression and Sunday school curriculum was a natural place to cut back, by the end of 1933, twelve courses had been published, and 13,366 copies sold to 131 churches in twenty-five states. A year later the sales had tripled. Soon, Gospel Light had overflowed Mr. Engle's garage and taken over his house. Meanwhile, Henrietta kept writing. Four years later, the four partners in the enterprise opened their new location: 1443 North Vine Street, two blocks from the famous corner of Hollywood and Vine. By 1937, a quarter of a million books had been sold.

Henrietta Mears next tackled worker training. She made reservations for two hundred people at a popular cafeteria in downtown Los Angeles. Hundreds more appeared; many ate while standing. More invitations to lecture and teach came to Miss Mears. She wanted to sell her audiences on "the Romance" of Sunday schools and Christian education. "Do you realize the vast potential you face every time you face your classes? Who knows the future of your pupils, but God?"[14]

Meanwhile, the Sunday school at Hollywood exploded. In 1928, 450 were enrolled; in 1930, the enrollment stood at 4,500. Because of the Depression, the church could not expand its facilities, and every nook and cranny had to be used. Miss Mears said, "I guess the Lord didn't give us an educational plant for years in order to prove that it isn't buildings out of which a Sunday school is to be created, but rather a program that presents Jesus Christ."[15]

Although other churches had "opening exercises" to begin the Sunday school, Henrietta planned worship. She insisted that even the youngest child could be taught to worship.

Henrietta Mears believed that wherever we are is holy ground. She stressed that we must "begin our Christian life, our Christian ministry, *where we are,* and let God lead from that moment on."[16] Since her address was Hollywood, it was natural that her interest would include the entertainment industry. J. Edwin Orr wrote that her heart "ached" for Hollywood, and she began praying for an opportunity.

Soon, Henrietta opened her home to a group of actors and actresses for what eventually became the Hollywood Christian Group. Well-known entertainers studied the Bible, prayed, and testified. Ruth Graham, wife of Billy Graham, told about attending one of the meetings where one particular actress shared with the group.

"I sat there like the Chief of Pharisees. Who did this woman think she was? Especially in light of some of the roles she had played. But Miss Mears was muttering, 'Bless her heart. I just love that girl! She is the dearest thing!' "[17]

However, the greatest contribution Henrietta Mears made was in the college department. It was not uncommon to have three hundred or more students from UCLA, USC, and other campuses in Southern California in her class on Sunday mornings, Sunday night fellowships, and Wednesday night prayer meetings. Baldwin said, "She had courage to venture out into difficult realms of thought and doctrine even if she couldn't fully comprehend them." Naturally, that courage "attracted the growing minds of her young people."[18] She was never too busy to hear their questions or struggles.

The class became her first love. Her Sunday mornings were straight lecture, while Wednesday night sessions were devoted to a group approach. Sunday nights offered forums, panels, and programs. She organized teams to visit jails, camps, college dormitories, and hospitals. After sessions, students loved to stay and talk and sing and snack. Miss Mears was usually off praying or counseling with someone. She had a most patient custodian, who always locked the college chapel last. Sometimes, after waiting, he would "encourage" students to leave by turning out the lights, but Mears was known to pray and counsel in the darkness. Henrietta was usually the last to leave; there was always one more student to talk to.

It is hardly surprising that out of this group over four hundred collegians became full-time Christian ministers. On her world tours, there were numerous conversations that began, "You probably don't remember me, but I was in your college department years ago and it was there I dedicated my life to Christ." It was said that she could fly into any major airport in the world and find someone she had influenced.[19]

The college group was serious. More than once she said, "Young people, I want you to think about what you are going to do with your lives. What are you living for? When you come to the last days God allows you on this earth, will you be satisfied?"[20]

She wanted more than spiritual gobbledygook that would attract college students. College students will be college students, but there was Teacher to bring them to a more Christ-centered emphasis. She could be firm.

> This has been the most ridiculous testimony time I think I have ever heard. All we have been talking about is silly little things that don't amount to a hill of beans! Have we lost sight of why we are here? There hasn't been one word about winning the nations for Christ. How about these great campuses in this area? Hasn't anything been done out at UCLA this week? Hasn't anyone witnessed to a student at USC? God weeps over these lost students, and we come here to talk about trifles.[21]

Henrietta Mears loved the outdoors. She also knew the value of getting students "away from it all." "God must have time to talk to people. In a city a person may hear one or two sermons a week, but at camp he is face to face with God for seven days."[22] After taking her youth and college students to Mount Hermon, near San Francisco, a thousand-mile round trip, she longed for a place closer to Hollywood. She found that in the mountains near San Bernardino where she founded the Forest Home Christian Conference Center and organized the College Briefing

Conferences, for students not only from her church, but from all over the nation. Her word for those conferences was *decision*. "If you place people in an atmosphere where they feel close to God and then challenge them with His Word, they will make decisions."[23]

Each conference had three emphases: (1) the acceptance of Christ as Savior and Lord; (2) the growth of the Christian; and (3) world vision. To Forest Home, she invited the best speakers in the world. She once personally invited C. S. Lewis, the British scholar and writer.

"But what would I have to contribute?" he asked. "All I have to contribute is my books, and you can read those for yourselves."

Henrietta Mears wasn't familiar with the word *no*. In fact, she argued that *failure* was not in the vocabulary of Christians.

"Then why don't you just come over and read to us your books? It would be a very great pleasure for us and a contribution just having you there."

"What! Do you mean to say you can't *read* in America?" he laughed. Miss Mears enjoyed his "no." All she could get from the noted writer was "Maybe, someday."[24]

In 1948, she invited a young preacher, unknown in church circles, to speak. Some people counseled her against the selection: He was not from an established church; he was young; some suggested he was unorthodox.

The speaker was having doubts of his own: Could he believe the Bible was true, in total? He had a crusade scheduled to begin in a few weeks in Los Angeles and was overwhelmed with his grappling.

He arrived at Forest Home early and that gave him several hours to talk to Miss Mears. Although his sermons that week were powerful, still he struggled with his own commitment. He often sat by a fish pond with Dr. J. Edwin Orr, discussing his struggles and the lack of power in his preaching.

Dr. Orr counseled him, but ultimately the young man walked the woods by himself. In the night, he reaffirmed his faith in the God of the Scriptures and prayed for God's strength in his life and on his preaching.

Someone has said that because the elevation of Forest Home is so high and therefore closer to heaven, it is easier for prayers to be answered. That young man came down from the mountain and opened his crusade in Los Angeles, and the world has never been the same.

The young man was Billy Graham.[25]

"I doubt if any other woman outside my wife and my mother has had such a marked influence [as Henrietta Mears]. Her gracious spirit, her devotional life, her steadfastness on the simple gospel, and her knowledge of the Bible have been a continual inspiration and amazement to me. She is certainly one of the greatest Christians I have ever known."[26]

That could be the testimony of countless other leaders influenced by Henrietta Mears, such as Bill Bright, founder of Campus Crusade for Christ. Dr. Mears's home, across from the UCLA campus, was always open to collegians. Bill and Vonette Bright launched their work from there, and they lived for almost a decade with Miss Mears.

Henrietta Mears outlasted three pastors at Hollywood Presbyterian. Dr. Louis Evans once said, "Whatever would I do without Miss Mears?"[27]

But the years of wearing so many hats so devotedly had drained her. Now she considered retirement. But how could she retire? There was still so much yet to be done. Finally, Ethel Baldwin said, she realized that God did not intend for her to retire.[28] Her death in 1961 was a "slipping" through a veil that she had taught across the years was "so very, very thin." She had risen early and prayed; she had prayed late. "It was nothing to her to meet her Lord alone, for she had often done so. This time she just went with Him." On her desk were the notes on several projects yet to be completed.

What Characterized the Unique Ministry of Henrietta Mears?

Henrietta Mears kept so much going that when she died it took three full-time people to replace her. What made Henrietta Mears such a special servant and such an influence on men like Billy Graham and Bill Bright?

Her commitment to Scripture. It might be said that the Bible was the only book for Henrietta Mears. After she had developed a reputation as a counselor, people would ask, "What does Miss Mears say?" Her retort was always, "What does the Bible say?"

One of her books is *What the Bible is All About*, with more than 3 million copies in print. She believed the Bible could be taught. "I have discovered that if the Bible is taught the way it should be it will be like a powerful magnet drawing [people] unto the Lord Jesus Christ! What a supremely superb Textbook we have!"[29]

Why then is the Bible so hard to study? Why didn't God make it plainer? From her background as a science teacher, she answered, "If God made coal for fuel, why did He not put it on the top of the ground instead of burying it deep underneath the surface?"[30]

The key to developing an understanding was to accept the wholeness. "Don't suppose reading little scraps can ever be compensation for doing deep and consecutive work on the Bible itself. We must get back to the Book and then we will not tolerate" poor teaching.[31]

She urged her students, regardless of their age, "*Read* it to be wise. *Believe* it to be safe. *Practice* it to be holy."[32]

Teaching so many university students and young professionals kept her on her toes, biblically. The contradictions were always argued. "Oh," she counseled, "if . . . you come across something in the Scriptures that in your limited knowledge you do not understand just then, lay the item aside temporarily and go on. Later on in your study, and in spiritual maturity, you will find the solution."[33]

Her commitment to teaching. Henrietta was a skilled writer, administrator, and counselor, but she lived to teach. After thirty years in Hollywood, she prayed, "Lord, as long as you see fit to keep me in that college department, you must make me attractive to those young people, and you must give me the message for this day and age that you want them to have."[34] She developed five goals for teaching:

- Help young people see themselves in a moral mirror.

- Help young people to see themselves as they really are and to overcome cynicism.

- Encourage them to find the highest motivations for their lives.

• Encourage them to make decisions.

• Assist them to see that God has a blueprint for their lives.[35]

What is a teacher? "God's man, in God's place, doing God's work, in God's way, for God's glory."[36]

Teachers must have something to say rather than having to say something. Mears asked, (1) Do I study the lesson thoroughly myself so that I can understand it? (2) Am I doing all I can to help my pupils understand the lesson and retain it in their memories? (3) Do I have them try to deduce their own applications from what they have heard? and (4) Does my teaching really influence their lives, or does it seem dull and removed from their immediate interests?[37]

One of the reasons why she counseled extensively was to be aware of the interests of her students.

Her commitment to individuals. Miss Mears lived by a "one-time" philosophy. "You never know when someone will be there in the audience for the first and only time." Moreover, she practiced that herself. "You will never have a second chance at a vast number of those to whom you minister." Every teaching experience had to be excellent.[38]

Henrietta Mears loved everyone who came into her life. Love was not some abstract theory. Whatever she was doing, she put aside to deal with a counselee. Once a boy appeared on Henrietta's doorstep pleading with her sister, Margaret, to see her. "I must see Miss Mears for fifteen minutes."

She reluctantly gave in: "Remember, *fifteen minutes!*"
Five hours later he emerged.

In another case a woman committed a crime but while on bail became a Christian. She served her time in jail, came out, and came to services at First Presbyterian, lonely, afraid of being rejected, hurt. Out of all those people who clamored for Henrietta's time, Miss Mears found the woman in the entryway and offered her love and some words of warm welcome.[39] It was a story that could be repeated many times. She always spotted visitors. She reminded her workers, "It is easier to get visitors than to keep them."[40]

Ruth Graham observed, "Some of us talk about love, but Miss Mears loves. No wonder God uses her."[41] One of her convictions was this statement: "I will make it easy for anyone to come to me with the deepest experiences of his inner life not by urging, but by sympathy and understanding. I will never let anyone think I am disappointed in him."[42]

"I am overwhelmed with the possibility that here may be a Martin Luther, or a John Knox, or a Calvin, or a Carey. Every Sunday morning I realize that I am facing the most important people in the world. Those who are stepping into my Sunday school class today may be stepping out tomorrow to become leaders of nations."[43]

No wonder so many people wanted to be around Henrietta Mears. Not everyone agreed with her investment of energy in certain people. More than once her counselees were called scoundrels, worthless. Her answer? "I have *never* considered anyone worthless."[44]

A commitment to developing leaders. Miss Mears loved talented people. She loved to see people discover things she had not seen. Never one to be threatened by the talents of others, she applauded their courage to tackle a new field. "I never discourage anyone from doing anything." Everyone had *some* potential for leadership. Henrietta Mears chose people not for what they were, but for what through God's grace they could *become*. She encouraged them with her enthusiasm and confidence and she made every resource, including herself and her time, available.[45]

However, Miss Mears would not let leaders coast. When they accomplished one goal creditably, she pushed them for bigger and better things, and she pushed them beyond any capacity they dreamed possible. She didn't let them "repeat a success but pushed them into something new and more challenging."[46]

A commitment to singleness. Hollywood was never boring while the two Mears sisters lived there. They were a team. Margaret made it possible for Henrietta to give herself so fully to ministry.

Margaret ran their home, paid the bills, did the shopping, and bought all of Henrietta's clothes, even the outrageous hats. Henrietta never had to give a thought as long as Margaret was alive to what she "should eat, drink, or wherewithal she would be clothed." Margaret never married, for she thought her first duty was to Henrietta.

Margaret sometimes ran interference for her sister; when Henrietta's ideas became impractical, Margaret intervened. She entertained Henrietta's collegians with her "views" on everything from trends in women's clothing, to the conduct of the Korean War, to the current status of UCLA football. Baldwin noted, "She kept their feet on the ground, as much as her sister kept their hearts in the sky."[47]

On December 20, 1951, Margaret suffered a stroke; she died two days later. It was a terrible loss, especially at Christmastime. Henrietta stayed busy. "I've been counseling others for so long and telling them that in a time of great loss and grief they must keep going, they mustn't quit, they must live moment by moment; so can I do less than what I have counseled others to do? Should I expect any less of myself than I have expected of others?"[48] Always the Teacher.

Henrietta modeled singleness to thousands of college students. She insisted that choosing a mate was one of life's greatest decisions. When collegians asked why she had not married, she answered because she had not lived in the same dispensation as the Apostle Paul. Moreover, she had never found anyone, in this age, to match him, although she kept looking. Once when teaching about the woman at the well who had had five husbands, Henrietta quipped, "Now she must have been a real glamour girl. She could get five husbands and I couldn't get one."[49]

Her singleness had been determined years before, on a spring Minnesota night. She had met a young banker, a graduate of Dartmouth, tall, handsome, and dark-haired. Yet, she sensed something missing in their relationship.

Oh, he admired her religious convictions; they could marry and she could do her thing religiously. He would live his faith; she would live hers. There was no question that Henrietta wanted a home; she loved children and entertaining. Yet, she decided that marrying this man would be like a home where the husband ate in the dining room each evening, and the wife in the kitchen. No fellowship.

Henrietta Mears prayed: "Lord, You have made me the way I am. I love a home, I love security, I love children, and I love him. Yet I feel that marriage under these conditions would draw me away from You. I surrender Lord, even this, and I leave it in Thy hands. Lead me, Lord, and strengthen me. You have promised to fulfill all my needs. I trust in Thee."[50]

Did the Lord fail her? No. Years later, having counseled hundreds about the decision to marry, she said,

The marvelous thing has been . . . that the Lord has always given me a beautiful home; He has given me thousands of children; the Lord has supplied everything in my life and I've never felt lonely. . . . I've never missed companionship. Through one experience after another the Lord has shown me that He had something peculiar and special for me to do. After I went through that final door, where it was just the Lord and myself, I've gone out into wide open spaces of people and things and excitement, and life has been an adventure. It has been a tremendous thing to see how the Lord has filled my life so abundantly with all these things and I just want to witness to the fact that wherever the Lord puts you, if He puts you on an island of the sea some place with Himself, He absolutely satisfies you.[51]

That caused a lot of women to consider the single life. Miss Mears dismissed such thinking. "Nonsense. The Lord intends for you to marry. . . ." But she added, "It has pleased me to know that they have been able to see my happiness and my complete satisfaction in the life that the Lord has given me."[52]

Her collegians called it "the will of God." The fear many had that God would destroy their personalities, their dreams, their ambitions. Miss Mears tried to help them see God as the Giver/Designer of their personalities.

"Young people are afraid that God will come to the fireplace and put out the fire, take the violin and break the strings instead of realizing that He will increase the fire on the hearth, and make more beautiful music on the strings of the violin."[53]

Simply, Miss Mears believed and taught that "God wants us to know His will even more than we want to know it." And what about while we wait to know His will? Henrietta Mears taught that you worked while you waited. She had hard words for people who did too much "waiting on the Lord."[54] She added, "No matter where I am, the Lord never intended me to be an observer."[55] Always a participant.

Some folks believed that Miss Mears had some special system; she was constantly asked about how she managed to get it all done. "The key is one word—work. Webster spells it, W-O-R-K, and it means just what he says it does. Wishful thinking will never take the place of hard work."[56]

Henrietta Mears learned to "take" time. She urged her students, her leaders to take time to be pleasant, to be polite, to be thoughtful. *Time.*

Her family was always concerned that she would over-work, or suffer an early death. She dismissed such thinking with the observation that "work won't kill you, but being frustrated about what you are supposed to do next will. How wonderful to know that you are in the place where God wants you."[57]

"You don't know what you can do until you try," she often told her collegians. A principle she lived by, too.

Who would have thought that single schoolteacher from Minnesota could have been so successful, two blocks from Hollywood and Vine?

One woman made an incredible difference for the good. Her own words said it best, "Many are called but few are choice."[58]

But ultimately her work has never ended. Her innovations in curriculum have impacted every Sunday school classroom in America. Gospel Light has supplied materials to over forty thousand churches in eighty languages.

One year before she died, she founded GLINT, Gospel Literature International, to complete her work. Henrietta Mears had "hiked in rhino-infested jungles in Africa, climbed mountains in Formosa, and walked amid the dying in India—all in order to obtain a better world view— to clarify the vision God put in her heart to reach a world with the gospel of Jesus Christ."[59]

GLINT's purpose, as defined by Miss Mears, is to facilitate the development of Bible teaching curricula in national churches. To date, curricula have been adapted, translated, and published in more than one hundred countries.

Afterword

Every age of every culture has had those who strive for some kind of meaning beyond just existing and surviving. There seems to be a profound universal need for humans to believe in something outside themselves.[1]

George Gallup, Jr.

For a long time I wondered if *Movers and Shapers* would ever be published. Why devote so much of my research and writing time to individuals whose names have little or no recognition in a celebrity-conscious society?

Even my friends and colleagues in writing cautioned against the project. They reminded me of the odds against publication of collective biography. Simply, biography of dead heroes isn't the easiest way to best-sellerdom. Yet, I kept reading and writing, almost seduced by this project.

Now you have read *Movers and Shapers*. I feel almost like one of the actors in Perry Mason. Remember when Della says to Perry, "The jury's in"? The verdict, please.

How have you reacted to my "friends": Lillian, Eartha, Lottie, Belle, Corrie, David, Henrietta, Phillips, and Luther?

It might be easy for you to say, "that was then; this is now," to elaborate a list of reasons why these movers couldn't make the same contribution today.

Or you might have read this book for entertainment. Perhaps you've enjoyed it. Yet you remain the same person who began the book.

Or perhaps you are aware that this book hasn't been a coincidence. You've gone back and reread certain parts. You've underlined certain sentences. You found yourself putting down the book for a while to think.

If you have read *Movers and Shapers*, perhaps there is a hunger within you for what I shall call "something more," for that added dimension to life.

The author of Hebrews pleads, "Therefore, since we are surrounded by such a great cloud of witnesses, let us throw off everything that hinders and the sin that so easily entangles, and let us run with perseverance the race *marked out for us*" (italics mine; Hebrews 12:1 NIV).

Lillian, Eartha, Lottie, Belle, Corrie, David, Henrietta, Phillips, and Luther have finished their race—all because they fixed their eyes on Jesus. Paul invites you to do the same thing. "Let us fix our eyes on Jesus, the author and perfector of our faith . . ." (Hebrews 12:2 NIV).

Some would argue that life is composed of great moments, great intersections, turning points; that if one carefully reads a person's life, one could discover the "aha" point.

I contend the opposite. After these years of research on movers and shapers, I have to believe that life is composed of small moments—often unrecognized for any hint of significance—when we say, as they say in Kentucky, "Keep on, keeping on." Success in life is a network of small moments in which we say yes to the best and no to the cheap.

The nineteenth-century English writer Edmund Burke wrote about the value of "little platoons"—private, voluntary groups of people who shape the conscience and attitudes of a society more than big government. I believe that the movers and shapers I've written about were part of God's great platoon for the redemption of humanity and society. While I have tried to trace their significance, this is not the final report. There remains a morning when God will complete the story.

Even a casual reading of the morning newspaper, a casual listening of the evening network news, reminds us of the great needs of our society. We need volunteers for a "little platoon" of single adults willing to take their places, willing to make a difference.

As I sat in libraries, reading, I often wondered, *Who will take their places?*

Life cannot be lived without heroes. People are often more inspired by a person's way of life than by his or her words. My purpose was not to set up these movers and shapers as models against which to judge your singleness and spirituality. But it is a confession of my conviction that we have drunk too deeply from the shallow streams of celebrity-ism.

These nine movers and shapers, in Lewis Smede's words, "embroidered the tapestry of human history by their inspired lives." There were hundreds more I could have chosen. And there are those who are now "moving and shaping." As Smedes observed, there are

. . . thousands of inspired people whose messages never get beyond their own neighborhoods. Maybe your uncle or your grandfather, or you. These are people worth listening to if only because of their brief time in a shadowy world they burn a candle of moral excellence to light up life a little for the rest of us. They leave us memories of noble choices when obedience was bought with the price of pain.[2]

I'm convinced that the movers and shapers of the past and of the present help us ordinary people make obedience a reality.

I would close with an observation from someone who read this manuscript in rough form and saw possibilities: *"God has no set formula for who He uses. He takes our failures and makes successes. And some people die not knowing what their influence to future generations is."*

Simply, God "had" Lillian and Henrietta and Corrie and Phillips and Lottie and Belle and David and Eartha and Luther and He *has* you.

Dare to be a mover and shaper in your zip code.

Dare to carry on the spirit of these movers and shapers.

Dare to carry on the vision of these movers and shapers.

Dare to carry on by holding to the ideals and high standards of these movers and shapers.

Dare to carry on the most common characteristic of these nine, their strong dependence on God.

"What doth the Lord require of thee?" asked the prophet Micah. His answer? "To do justly, and to love mercy, and to walk humbly with thy God" (Micah 6:8).

Source Notes

Chapter 1: Lillian Trasher

1. Beth Prim Howell, *Lady on a Donkey* (New York: Doubleday, 1960), p. 22.
2. *Letters From Lillian* (Springfield, Missouri: Division of Foreign Missions, Assembly of God, 1983), p. 98.
3. Ibid., pp. 98, 99.
4. Ibid., p. 12.
5. Howell, *Lady*, pp. 102–104.
6. Ibid.
7. "Christian Orphanage in Egypt Thrives After 74 Years," *Dallas Morning News* (December 15, 1985), p. 49A.
8. Howell, *Lady*, p. 113.
9. Ibid., p. 156.
10. *Letters*, p. 28.
11. Ibid., p. 23.
12. Ibid., p. 32.
13. Howell, *Lady*, p. 160.
14. *Letters*, p. 35; Jerome Beatty, "Nile Mother," *American Magazine* (June 1939), p. 33.
15. *Letters*, p. 51.

16. Ibid., p. 110.
17. Ibid., p. 49.
18. Ibid., p. 85.
19. Ibid., pp. 119, 120.
20. Ibid., p. 111.
21. Ibid., p. 96.
22. Ibid., p. 16.
23. Ibid., p. 35.
24. Ibid., p. 104.
25. Ibid.
26. Adele Dalton, "Women of Faith: They Called Her Mama" (January 1983), document in archives, Assembly of God, Springfield, Missouri.

Chapter 2: Phillips Brooks

1. Alexander V. G. Allen, *Phillips Brooks: Memories of His Life with Extracts From His Letters and Notebooks* (New York: E. P. Dutton, 1907), p. 575.
2. Alexander V. G. Allen, *Life and Letters of Phillips Brooks*, III (New York: E. P. Dutton, 1900), p. 90.
3. Ibid., p. 143.
4. Ibid., p. 163.
5. Ibid., p. 330.
6. Ibid., p. 338.
7. Ibid., p. 341.
8. Ibid., p. 339.
9. Ibid., p. 347.
10. Ibid.
11. Ibid., p. 359.
12. Ibid., p. 365.
13. Ibid., p. 369.
14. Ibid., p. 372.
15. Ibid., p. 375.
16. Ibid., p. 449.
17. Ibid., p. 463.
18. Ibid., p. 467.
19. Ibid.
20. Ibid., p. 535.

21. Ibid., p. 538.

22. Ibid., pp. 476, 477.

23. Ibid., p. 635.

24. Allen, *Memories*, p. 299.

25. Ibid., p. 503.

26. Ibid., p. 302.

27. Ibid., p. 561.

28. Thomas F. Chilcote, Jr., ed., *The Excellence of Our Calling* (New York: E. P. Dutton, 1954), p. 16.

29. Allen, *Memories*, p. 342.

30. Charles Allen Dinsmore, "Phillips Brooks," *Dictionary of American Biography*, Vol. II (New York: Charles Scribner's, 1961), p. 87.

31. Allen, *Memories*, p. 471.

32. Phillips Brooks, *Lectures on Preaching* (New York: E.P. Dutton, 1877), p. 5.

33. Allen, *Memories*, p. 306.

34. Ibid., p. 311.

35. Chilcote, *Excellence*, p. 14.

36. Brooks, *Lectures*, p. 107.

37. William Scarlett, ed., *Phillips Brooks: Selected Sermons* (New York: E. P. Dutton, 1950), p. 7.

38. Allen, *Letters*, p. 247.

39. Allen, *Memories*, p. 604.

40. Chilcote, *Excellence*, p. 18.

41. Allen, *Memories*, p. 578.

42. Ibid., p. 488.

43. Ibid., p. 466.

44. Ibid.

45. Ibid., p. 567.

46. Ibid., p. 175.

47. Ibid., p. 342.

48. Ibid., p. 631.

Chapter 3: Belle Bennett

1. Mrs. Jesse Lee Cuninggim, "A Brief Review of the Life of Belle Harris Bennett," Founder's Day ceremonies, Scarritt College, Nashville, Tennessee, May 15, 1952, p. 7.

2. J. L. Cuninggim, "Brief Biographical Sketches: Belle Bennett," Archives, Scarritt College, item dated June 1942.

3. R. W. MacDonell, *Belle Harris Bennett* (Nashville: Board of Missions, Methodist Episcopal Church, South, 1928), p. 31.

4. Ibid.

5. Alice Cobb, *A History of Scarrit College* (Nashville: Scarritt College, 1987), p. 15.

6. Ibid., p. 16.

7. MacDonell, p. 56; J. L. Cuninggim, p. 8.

8. Mrs. Cuninggim, p. 9.

9. Cobb, p. 11.

10. Mabel K. Howell, "The Service Motive—Scarritt College, 1892–1942," typewritten manuscript, Archives, Scarritt College, p. 35; Cobb, p. 21.

11. Ibid., quoting "An Appeal for Two Hundred Women," Women's Missionary Activity, 7 (1890), pp. 12–18.

12. Emily K. Olmstead, *Intimate Glimpses of Belle H. Bennett* (Nashville: Belle H. Bennett Memorial Committee of the Women's Missionary Council, Methodist Episcopal Church, South, 1923), p. 26.

13. MacDonell, p. 125.

14. Mrs. Cuninggim, p. 13.

15. Mary Christine DeBardeleben, *Lambuth-Bennett Book of Remembrance* (Nashville: Publishing House of the Methodist Episcopal Church, South, 1922), p. 89.

16. Mrs. Cuninggim, p. 16.

17. MacDonell, p. 44.

18. Mrs. R. W. MacDonell, "Belle H. Bennett—Leader Among Women," *Methodist Quarterly Review* (1923), p. 4.

19. MacDonell, pp. 246–247.

20. Ibid., p. 243.

21. Ibid., p. 254.

22. Ibid., p. 248.

23. Ibid., p. 254.

24. Carolyn L. Stapleton, "Belle Harris Bennett: Model of Holistic Christianity," *Methodist History*, 21 (April 1983), p. 131.

25. Olmstead, *Intimate Glimpses*, p. 18.

26. Stapleton, *Belle Bennett*, p. 135.

27. MacDonell, p. 124.

28. Ibid., p. 261.

Source Notes

29. Ibid., p. 124.
30. Ibid., p. 90.
31. Stapleton, *Belle Bennett*, p. 133.
32. DeBardeleben, *Lambuth-Bennett Book*, p. 305.

Chapter 4: David Brainerd

1. John Wesley, *The Works of Reverend John Wesley* (London: Wesleyan Conference Office, 1872), p. 328.
2. David Wynbeek, *David Brainerd: Beloved Yankee* (Grand Rapids: Eerdmans, 1961), p. 30.
3. Ibid., p. 31.
4. Jonathan Edwards, ed., *The Life and Diary of David Brainerd* (Chicago: Moody, 1949), pp. 75, 76.
5. Ibid., p. 77.
6. Ibid.
7. Ibid., p. 86.
8. Ibid., p. 87.
9. Ibid., p. 89.
10. Ibid., p. 90.
11. Ibid., p. 98.
12. Ibid., p. 99.
13. Wynbeek, *Beloved Yankee*, p. 99.
14. Edwards, *Life and Diary*, p. 105.
15. Ibid., p. 113.
16. Ibid., pp. 119, 120.
17. Ibid., p. 120.
18. Ibid., pp. 122–124; Wynbeek, *Beloved Yankee*, p. 48.
19. Edwards, *Life and Diary*, p. 124.
20. Wynbeek, *Beloved Yankee*, p. 67.
21. J. M. Sherwood, ed., *Memoirs of Reverend David Brainerd* (New York: Funk and Wagnalls, 1884), pp. xxvii.
22. Wynbeek, *Beloved Yankee*, p. 64.
23. Ibid., p. 68.
24. Ibid., p. 86; Edwards, *Life and Diary*, p. 163.
25. Wynbeek, *Beloved Yankee*, p. 93.
26. Edwards, *Life and Diary*, p. 175.
27. Wynbeek, *Beloved Yankee*, p. 150.
28. Edwards, *Life and Diary*, p. 208.

29. Ibid., p. 212.
30. Wynbeek, *Beloved Yankee*, pp. 155, 157.
31. Ibid., p. 162.
32. Edwards, *Life and Diary*, pp. 222, 223.
33. Wynbeek, *Beloved Yankee*, p. 239.
34. Sherwood, *Memoirs*, p. 335.
35. Ibid., p. 340.
36. Ibid., p. xlvii.
37. Ibid., p. 340.
38. Ibid., p. 27.
39. Ibid., p. 342.
40. Thomas Brainerd, *The Life of John Brainerd* (Philadelphia: Presbyterian Publishing Company, 1865), p. 89.

Chapter 5: Charlotte Digges "Lottie" Moon

1. Catherine B. Allen, *The New Lottie Moon Story* (Nashville: Broadman, 1980), p. 288.
2. Ibid., p. 33.
3. Ibid., p. 34.
4. Ibid., p. 35.
5. Ibid., pp. 38–39.
6. Una Roberts Lawrence, *Lottie Moon* (Nashville: Sunday School Board of the Southern Baptist Convention, 1927), p. 50.
7. Ibid., p. 62.
8. Allen, *New Lottie Moon*, p. 68.
9. Lawrence, *Lottie Moon*, p. 63.
10. Allen, *New Lottie Moon*, p. 70; Lawrence, *Lottie Moon*, p. 65. *See also* Rosemary Radford Reuther and Rosemary Skinner Kelley, *Women and Religion in America*, Volume 1 (San Francisco: Harper and Row, 1981), p. 247; Eliza Chester, *The Unmarried Woman* (New York: Dodd, Mead, 1892), p. 89.
11. Allen, *New Lottie Moon*, p. 88.
12. Ibid., p. 96.
13. Ibid., p. 98.
14. Lawrence, *Lottie Moon*, p. 82.
15. Leon McBeth, *Women in Baptist Life* (Nashville: Broadman, 1980), p. 91.
16. Allen, *New Lottie Moon*, p. 93.

17. Ibid., p. 71.
18. McBeth, *Women in Baptist Life*, p. 93.
19. Allen, *New Lottie Moon*, p. 142.
20. Ibid., p. 256.
21. Ibid., p. 158.
22. Ibid., p. 101.
23. Ibid., p. 170.
24. Ibid., p. 137.
25. Lawrence, *Lottie Moon*, p. 92; Allen, *New Lottie Moon*, p. 138.
26. Lawrence, *Lottie Moon*, p. 247.
27. Allen, *New Lottie Moon*, pp. 217, 218.
28. Ibid., pp. 100, 223.
29. Ibid., p. 224.
30. Ibid., pp. 201, 202.
31. Ibid., p. 287.
32. Ibid., p. 132.
33. Ibid., p. 133.
34. Ibid., p. 160.
35. Ibid., p. 246.
36. Ibid., p. 87.
37. Ibid., p. 247.
38. Lawrence, *Lottie Moon*, p. 67.
39. Allen, *New Lottie Moon*, p. 139.
40. Ibid., p. 278.
41. Ibid., p. 158.
42. Lawrence, *Lottie Moon*, p. 276.
43. Allen, *New Lottie Moon*, p. 278.
44. Ibid., p. 240.
45. Ibid., p. 238.

Chapter 6: Correman "Corrie" ten Boom

1. Corrie ten Boom, *Amazing Love* (Fort Washington, Pa.: Christian Literature Crusade, 1953), pp. 17–19.
2. "Corrie ten Boom Dies at Age 91," *Christianity Today*, 27 (May 20, 1983), pp. 52, 53; Corrie ten Boom with C. C. Carlson, *In My Father's House* (Old Tappan, N.J.: Revell, 1976), pp. 58, 59.
3. ten Boom, *Father's House*, pp. 114–116.
4. Ibid., pp. 36, 37.

5. Carole C. Carlson, *Corrie ten Boom: Her Life, Her Faith* (Old Tappan, N.J.: Revell, 1983), p. 58.

6. ten Boom, *Father's House*, p. 157.

7. Carlson, *Corrie ten Boom*, p. 53.

8. Pamela Rosewell, *The Five Silent Years of Corrie ten Boom* (Grand Rapids: Zondervan, 1986), p. 10.

9. Corrie ten Boom with John and Elizabeth Sherrill, *The Hiding Place* (Old Tappan, N.J.: Revell, 1971), p. 106.

10. Ibid.

11. Ibid.

12. *Christianity Today*, p. 54.

13. Carlson, *Corrie ten Boom*, pp. 118, 119.

14. Corrie ten Boom with Jamie Buckingham, *Tramp for the Lord* (Fort Washington, Pa.: Christian Literature Crusade, 1976), p. 37.

15. Ibid., p. 38.

16. Carlson, *Corrie ten Boom*, p. 144.

17. Ibid., p. 148.

18. Ibid., p. 183.

19. Interview with David Messenger, M.D., physician of Corrie ten Boom, LaMirada, California, July 17, 1987.

20. Carlson, *Corrie ten Boom*, p. 119.

21. Rosewell, *The Five Silent Years*, p. 14.

22. Carlson, *Corrie ten Boom*, p. 194.

23. Ibid.

24. Corrie ten Boom, *A Tramp Finds a Home* (Old Tappan, N.J.: Revell, 1978), p. 51.

25. ten Boom, *Amazing Love*, p. 32.

26. ten Boom, *Tramp for the Lord*, p. 128.

27. Ibid., p. 130.

28. Carlson, *Corrie ten Boom*, pp. 26, 27.

29. ten Boom, *Tramp for the Lord*, pp. 130, 131.

30. ten Boom, *Father's House*, pp. 62, 66.

31. Memorial Service for Corrie ten Boom, April 22, 1983, Santa Ana, California, published by Fleming H. Revell, 1983.

32. Ibid.

33. ten Boom, *Father's House*, p. 26.

34. Carlson, *Corrie ten Boom*, p. 16.

35. Rosewell, *The Five Silent Years*, p. 22.

36. Carlson, *Corrie ten Boom*, pp. 52, 53.

37. Ibid.
38. ten Boom, *Father's House*, p. 41.
39. Messenger interview.
40. Carlson, *Corrie ten Boom*, p. vii.
41. Carlson, *Corrie ten Boom*, p. 192; ten Boom, *Amazing Love*, p. 23.
42. *Tramp for the Lord*, pp. 107–108.
43. Carlson, *Corrie ten Boom*, p. 189.
44. Memorial service, p. 10.
45. Rosewell, *The Five Silent Years*, p. 69.
46. Ibid., p. 92.
47. ten Boom, *Hiding Place*, pp. 43–45.
48. ten Boom, *Father's House*, pp. 145, 146.
49. Messenger interview.
50. ten Boom, *Tramp for the Lord*, p. 57.
51. Carlson, *Corrie ten Boom*, p. 190.
52. Rosewell, *The Five Silent Years*, p. 25.
53. Carlson, *Corrie ten Boom*, p. 190.
54. ten Boom, *Father's House*, p. 192.
55. Ibid., pp. 152, 153.
56. Rosewell, *The Five Silent Years*, p. 157, italics mine.
57. Carlson, *Corrie ten Boom*, pp. 124, 125.
58. ten Boom, *Tramp for the Lord*, pp. 53–55.
59. Carlson, *Corrie ten Boom*, p. 142.

Chapter 7: Eartha Mary Magdalene White

1. Eugene Levy, *James Weldon Johnson: Black Leader/Black Voice* (Chicago: University of Chicago Press, 1973), p. 8.

2. *The Florida Times-Union* (November 11, 1966), p. 6.

3. James Robertson Ward, *Old Hickory's Town: An Illustrated History of Jacksonville* (Jacksonville: Florida Publishing Company, 1982), p. 183; Daniel L. Schafer, "Eartha M. White—The Early Years of a Jacksonville Humanitarian," unpublished biographical document, University of North Florida, Archives, dated May 1976, p. 20.

4. Barbara Ann Richardson, "A History of Blacks in Jacksonville, Florida, 1860–1895: A Social, Economic and Political Study, D.A. dissertation, Carnegie-Mellon University, 1975, p. 208.

5. Schafer, "The Early Years," p. 29.

6. "Eartha White," in *Notable American Women: The Modern Period: A Biographical Dictionary,* edited by Barbara Sicherman and Carol Hurd Green (Cambridge: Belknap Press, 1980), p. 727.

7. Eartha M. White to Mrs. J. E. Young, letter, Archives, University of North Florida (March 4, 1910).

8. Ibid.

9. Sicherman and Green, *Notable American Women,* p. 727.

10. Schafer, "The Early Years," p. 20.

11. Ibid., p. 31.

12. *Florida Times-Union* (November 11, 1966), p. 6.

13. Document, dated November 1, 1941, Archives, University of North Florida.

14. Schafer, "The Early Years," p. 25.

15. Sicherman and Green, *Notable American Women,* p. 727.

16. Ibid.

17. Harold Gibson, "My Most Unforgettable Character: Eartha White," *Reader's Digest* (December 1974), p. 127.

18. *Florida Times-Union* (March 4, 1910), p. 7.

19. *Florida Times-Union* (November 13, 1966), p. 7.

20. *Jacksonville Journal* (December 5, 1970), np.

21. Schafer, "The Early Years," p. 16.

22. *Florida Times-Union* (November 13, 1966), p. 7.

23. *Florida Times-Union* (no month, 1969), item in White's scrapbook, Archives.

24. *Florida Times-Union* (October 14, 1969), p. B-4.

Chapter 8: Luther Rice

1. Edwin B. Pollard and Daniel Gorden Stevens, *Luther Rice: Pioneer in Missions and Education* (Philadelphia: Judson, 1928), p. 4.

2. Ibid.

3. Evelyn Wingo Thompson, *Luther Rice: Believer in Tomorrow* (Nashville: Broadman, 1967), p. 12.

4. Pollard and Stevens, *Pioneer in Missions,* p. 5.

5. Thompson, *Believer in Tomorrow,* pp. 21, 22.

6. Ibid., pp. 23, 25.

7. James B. Taylor, *Memoir of Reverend Luther Rice,* second edition (Nashville: Broadman, 1841), pp. 31, 32.

Source Notes

8. Ibid., p. 33.

9. Pollard and Stevens, *Pioneer in Missions,* p. 9.

10. Thompson, *Believer in Tomorrow,* p. 38.

11. Ibid., pp. 38, 39.

12. Ibid., p. 52.

13. L. Woods, *A Sermon on the Ordination of Samuel Newell, Samuel Nott, Gordon Hall, Adoniram Judson and Luther Rice* (Boston: Samuel T. Armstrong, 1812), p. 33.

14. Ibid., pp. 27, 33.

15. Thompson, *Believer in Tomorrow,* p. 64.

16. Pollard and Stevens, *Pioneer in Missions,* pp. 18, 19.

17. Ibid., p. 21.

18. Taylor, *Memoir,* p. 120.

19. Pollard and Stevens, *Pioneer in Missions,* p. 24.

20. *Proceedings of the Baptist Convention for Mission Purposes,* Philadelphia: May, 1814, 1815, 1816, 1817 (Philadelphia: Ann Coles, 1817), p. 13.

21. Ibid., p. 31.

22. Thompson, *Believer in Tomorrow,* pp. 80, 81.

23. *Proceedings,* p. 145.

24. Clifton E. Olmstead, *History of Religion in the United States* (Englewood Cliffs, N.J.: Prentice-Hall, 1960), pp. 271, 272.

25. Ibid., p. 272.

26. Thompson, *Believer in Tomorrow,* pp. 117, 186.

27. Ibid., p. 186.

28. Taylor, *Memoir,* p. 266; Pollard and Stevens, *Pioneer in Missions,* p. 80.

29. Pollard and Stevens, *Pioneer in Missions,* p. 83.

30. Ibid., p. 85.

31. Thompson, *Memoir,* p. 193.

32. Pollard and Stevens, *Pioneer in Missions,* p. 109.

33. Ibid., p. 111; Thompson, *Memoir,* pp. 199, 200.

34. Pollard and Stevens, *Pioneer in Missions,* p. 53.

35. Thompson, *Memoir,* p. 101.

36. Pollard and Stevens, *Pioneer in Missions,* pp. 57, 58.

37. Ibid., pp. 106, 107.

Chapter 9: Henrietta Mears

1. Ethel May Baldwin and David Benson, *Henrietta Mears and How She Did It* (Ventura, Calif.: Regal, 1966), Foreword.
2. *The Vision Grows: Fifty Years, 1933–1983* (Ventura, Calif.: Gospel Light, 1983), p. 6.
3. Barbara Hudson Powers, *The Henrietta Mears Story* (Old Tappan, N.J.: Fleming Revell, 1965), p. 111.
4. Deborah Fero Young, "Her Faith Made a Difference: Henrietta Mears," *Reflections* (March–April 1982), p. 29.
5. Baldwin, *How She Did It*, p. 37.
6. Ibid.
7. Young, "Her Faith," p. 30.
8. Baldwin, *How She Did It*, p. 48.
9. Ibid., pp. 48–50.
10. Ibid., pp. 57, 58.
11. Powers, *Mears Story*, p. 32.
12. Baldwin, *How She Did It*, pp. 61, 62.
13. Ibid., p. 67.
14. Powers, *Mears Story*, p. 32.
15. Baldwin, *How She Did It*, pp. 77, 78.
16. Powers, *Mears Story*, p. 57.
17. J. Edwin Orr, *The Inside Story of the Hollywood Christian Group* (Grand Rapids: Zondervan, 1955), pp. 14, 15; Powers, *Mears Story*, p. 69.
18. Baldwin, *How She Did It*, p. 123.
19. Ibid., pp. 143, 130.
20. Ibid., p. 145.
21. Ibid., pp. 128, 129.
22. Ibid., p. 204.
23. Ibid., p. 209.
24. Powers, *Mears Story*, p. 20.
25. Baldwin, *How She Did It*, p. 252; Powers, *Mears Story*, p. 183; John Pollock, *Billy Graham* (New York: McGraw-Hill, 1966), pp. 53, 54.
26. Powers, *Mears Story*, Introduction.
27. Ibid., p. 138.
28. Baldwin, *How She Did It*, p. 276.
29. Eleanor L. Doan, ed., *431 Quotes From the Notes of Henrietta C. Mears* (Glendale, Calif.: Gospel Light, 1961), p. 41.

Source Notes

30. Ibid., p. 62.

31. Henrietta C. Mears, *What the Bible Is All About* (Ventura, Calif.: Gospel Light, 1983), p. 20.

32. Doan, *431 Quotes*, p. 62.

33. Powers, *Mears Story*, p. 58.

34. Baldwin, *How She Did It*, p. 259.

35. Ibid., pp. 324–328.

36. Doan, *431 Quotes*, p. 41.

37. Ibid.

38. Powers, *Mears Story*, p. 167.

39. Baldwin, *How She Did It*, p. 57.

40. Dorothy C. Haskin, *Christians You Would Like to Know* (Grand Rapids: Zondervan, 1954), p. 57.

41. Baldwin, *How She Did It*, pp. 104, 105.

42. Ibid., pp. 99, 100.

43. Ibid., pp. 288, 289.

44. Ibid., p. 340.

45. Powers, *Mears Story*, p. 159.

46. Ibid., p. 160.

47. Ibid., p. 121; Baldwin, *How She Did It*, p. 260.

48. Powers, *Mears Story*, p. 81.

49. Ibid., p. 114.

50. Ibid., pp. 115, 116.

51. Ibid.

52. Ibid.

53. Ibid., p. 75.

54. Ibid., pp. 63, 64.

55. Doan, *431 Quotes*, p. 26.

56. Ibid., p. 21.

57. Baldwin, *How She Did It*, p. 300.

58. Doan, *431 Quotes*, p. 3.

59. *The Vision Grows*, p. 11.

Afterword

1. George Gallup, Jr., and George O'Connor, *Who Do Americans Say That I Am?* (Philadelphia: Westminster, 1986), p. 15.

2. Lewis Smedes, *Choices: Making Right Decisions in a Complex World* (San Francisco: Harper and Row, 1986), p. 120.